STIR-FRIED MEMORIES

By Cherise Wyneken

A Whispering Angel Book

Stir-Fried Memories

Copyright © 2012 by Whispering Angel Books.

The stories contained in this memoir are based on the true, personal recollections of the author. Views expressed are solely that of the author. The publisher does not endorse any viewpoint over another.

Some of the stories have been previously published as the author has retained copyright to each piece. A complete list of previous publication credits can be found at the end of the book.

All rights reserved under International and Pan-American copyright conventions. No part of this book may be used or reproduced by any means, graphic, electronic, or mechanical including photocopying, recording, taping or by any storage retrieval system without written permission of the publisher except in the case of brief quotations embodied in critical reviews and articles.

ISBN 978-0-9841421-7-0

Whispering Angel Books
http://www.whisperingangelbooks.com

Printed in the United States of America

Whispering Angel Books is dedicated to publishing uplifting and inspirational works for its readers while donating a portion of its book sales to charitable organizations promoting physical, emotional, and spiritual healing. If you'd like to learn more about our books or our fundraising programs for your charity, please visit our website: www.whisperingangelbooks.com

MENU

Flavor – Personal Experience

Prologue iii
Carnival 1
Hard Times 4
California Bound 6
Torn From Place 12
Lazy Days 15
War Torn 17
Miss "H" 22
Paper Moon 24
Shoreline 27
Decision Time 29
"How Way Leads Onto Way" 33
The Pregnant Camper 37
First Born 39
Stir-fried Genes 41
Manifest 43
Perspectives 46
Dear Doctor 49
Prime Time 52
A Moving Event 56
Garage Sale 62
Crisis To Emancipation 64

Moving Along	67
Scattered Beads	69
One of These Days	72
One Small Step	77
How's My Backhand?	80
Mama's Move	83
Good-bye Again	90
What If?	93
Me and My Biopsy	95
I Bring My Book …	98
Fleeing Floyd	99
SPLAT!	102
Tide Pools	105

Color – Travel and Nature

A French Revolution	111
Florida Living	112
For the Birds	114
La Bomba	117
South to Kerala	120

Nutrition – Inspiration

"A Rose is a Rose is a Rose"	129
Back From the Brink	131
Catching the Ring	134
Making Babies	136
Mothering Works	138
Submit? To My Husband?	141
The Art of Receiving	142
The Fellowship of Women	144
This I Believe	146
Unseen Power	147

Fragrance – Humor

Almost There	153
A Matter of Fact	158
Close Encounters With Cars	159
No Score	164
Acknowledgements	166

PROLOGUE

Like a Chinese menu, "Stir-fried Memories" serves tasty morsels that appeal to a variety of interests. It is a collection of essays and personal experience pieces combined much like vegetables are mixed together in a wok for a tasty stir-fried meal, heaped with flavor, color, nutrition, and fragrance. It offers readers a taste of living through humor, travel, childhood, major moves, sickness, death, and family.

FLAVOR – PERSONAL EXPERIENCES

CARNIVAL

Mmmmm, I thought. Mama sure cooks good. I was sitting at the table day dreaming and stirring the hot soup she had made for lunch. No gourmet chef could make a tastier soup than Mama's "Early Vegetable." She would gather new shoots from her garden: tender peas, tiny carrots, potatoes, small beets – tops and all – and put them in a pot of chicken stock. She added a generous amount of cream and watched it turn sunset pink. Mama didn't serve it more than once or twice in the early spring. (By the time she decided to make soup again, the vegetables were mature and didn't taste the same).

Behind the fence, in a little shed, Mama kept several chickens. Once we owned a cow and later a goat. My cousin, Don, fed tin cans to Nanny and tormented her in other ways. One day she had enough and butted him into Mama's basket of frozen wash just taken from the clothesline. (Don learned his lesson – frozen long johns are sharp). Mama's favorite was her covey of pigeons. She called each by name and watched their love affairs as avidly as she read the dime romances. If she could bring herself to do it, she would turn the chicks into delicate pigeon pies for her special guests. They were just as tasty as her "Early Vegetable."

Mama and Daddy were talking and looking straight at me while I was daydreaming.

"Wake up, Katrinka," Daddy said. "I was telling you about a carnival coming soon."

"A carnival?"

"Yup. A carnival and more than that. It'll be a big to-do for the town's Diamond Jubilee. Rides and speeches and a big parade. It'll last three days!"

"Will I get to ride the merry-go-round?" I asked. "I don't have any money." Mama and Daddy had already thought of that.

"If you gather all the eggs, every day, we will give you half of them to sell. You can save your money for the carnival," Mama said.

I hated selling things. Sometimes when my brother, George, went off to scout camp I had to do his paper route. He always ordered extras and sold them on the street. I stashed them behind the Post Office door where they had been delivered in the first place. The only paper I would "sell" was to Uncle Dave's rival creamery. The owner had a standing order for Saturdays and paid with a jar of sour cream. Mama would make a pot of soup and johnny cake for supper that night. When the cornbread turned a golden brown she spread the sour cream on top, sprinkled it with sugar, and popped it back into the oven. The sugar and the cream turned into a crystal crust and filled the house with sweet and sour smells.

Now I had a reason to overcome my shyness. I vowed to earn enough money to sample every ride. Each time I sold some eggs to the general store I counted my coins and watched the stack grow along with my anticipation.

Everyone was getting ready. Even Daddy was growing a beard. Any man without one would be put inside the monkey cage on Main Street until he paid a fine. Mama didn't like it, but Daddy was the marshal. He had to keep the "law." He did look funny. His blue eyes twinkled as he thought about the coming fun.

****

Carnival day arrived at last.

"You kids can run along and watch the parade," said Mama. "I'll find you afterwards."

Daddy had left early to maintain law and order.

Could this be our town, I wondered as we approached Main Street.

It looked like a wonderland, with rides strung through the center like giant birds swooping and flying, and side shows lined along the curbs. There were flags and lights, balloons, and crowds of people walking in the summer air. One ticket bought three shots at the shooting gallery. Cotton candy floated on tall, paper cones like sunset cloud banks through the sky. Laughter pulsed with music from the band. A carousel of steeds rode in rings of captivating glee.

I found my friends and tried it all – even darts – although I never could throw straight. I was always the last one chosen for a team at school. "Do we have to have her on our team," the captain would complain. Today I tried again – hoping for a Kewpie doll – and failed.

Further down the street fire-eaters licked and lapped at flapping, flaming tongues and others dined on swords. Hawkers called in frenzy: "HUR -ee! HUR -ee! HUR - ee!" I looked up toward the stage and saw George with a snake drooped around his neck.

"Hi," he said when he came back down unscathed. "Did you see me?"

I made a face and shuddered.

"Come on," he said. "Let's ride the loop-de-loop."

As we stood in line I opened my purse to get my nickel. To my amazement there was nothing left. What was I to do tomorrow? How careless to spend all my money on the first day – after Mama and Daddy had let me have the eggs! A red-hot fire crept across my neck and ears.

"I don't want to ride the Loop-de-loop," I snapped.

I turned and ran away. Like a storm-wracked homing pigeon, I headed for Daddy's car parked on a side street. I curled into the dark back seat and washed my shame with tears. After an eternity, George came hunting for me.

"Oh, here you are," he said, peering through the window. "Mama and Daddy have been looking everywhere for you. Come on."

"Hurry, Katrinka," Daddy called from near the ferris wheel. "Come for a ride with me."

"I can't, Daddy. I spent all my money."

"Already? Well never mind. They gave me some free passes because I'm the marshal. You don't need your money."

Like a giant wave the wheel climbed into the night sky. It seemed to me we could touch the stars. When we reached the top it stopped. The seat swayed back and forth. I leaned over to look at the bright lights in the town below – too happy to be frightened.

HARD TIMES

Mama put the phone back on the hook. "It's Pa. He's fading fast. Ma says we'd better come."

"What's that mean?" I asked. "What's the matter with Grampa?"

"You wouldn't understand."

"Mastoid infection," George interjected.

"What's that?"

"See what I mean?" Mama said. "Run along and change your dress."

We chugged along the narrow gravel road in the Model A toward Aberdeen. Daddy had to move aside only once from the center ruts for an oncoming car. A bevy of golden pheasants took to wing from the ditch as the car passed them. Fields of wheat stretched below a blue cotton-balled sky. Everything seemed peaceful – except in my heart. I'd never been inside a hospital. What was happening to Grampa?

Grampa's high cheekbones accentuated the gauntness of his face. His wasting body showed in the sharpness of his nose and chin. The room was cold and white. White enamel covered the iron bedstead. His gown was white. The sheets were white. He seemed a ghost already.

He reached for Daddy's hand. "Promise me – you'll take care of Ma."

Daddy shook it in return. His duties started soon.

He moved his family in with Gramma. It wasn't home for me. The parlor spoke of Grampa's coffin where I had seen his warm brown eyes closed in cold sleep. The furniture was stiff and black. A long fringed scarf like an altar cloth covered the library table. An open Bible lay on top. Church seemed far more inviting to me than this funeral parlor. In the spring they converted the big house into flats and rented the downstairs. Gramma moved upstairs and Daddy took his family home.

Daddy lost his job as marshall when the local Republicans came into power. He turned once more to farming – watching the sky for clouds and rain. None came. Seeds shriveled. Dry earth cracked and crumbled into dust. It blew through cracks and crevices. Coated furniture and floors. Mama tried in vain to keep things clean. George and I wrote our names on the dusty sills. My body left a pattern on the bed where I napped.

If a field of corn or wheat managed to mature it was eaten by swarms of grasshoppers. Like big black clouds covering the sun they approached a field and devoured it in one sitting.

The W.P.A. offered Daddy jobs from time to time and gave away sacks of food to people without work.

"You kids could use some of those oranges," Mama said one day. "George – whyn't you go down and get us some. We've got a right to our share, too."

She saw the look of humiliation on his face as he explained how he'd had to stand in line. She never made him go again. Between the garden and the animals we managed.

Sometimes Daddy went with groups of men to North Dakota or Canada following the threshers. He would be gone for weeks. He even tried to make money, raising fryers for the market. When the chicks had grown enough Daddy took them into Aberdeen to sell. The going price didn't meet his initial investment so he brought them home again. Mama served fried chicken often that spring.

"Cock-a-doodle-doo!" Daddy crowed when we sat down to eat.

One cold autumn Saturday Frankie and my parents packed a picnic lunch. They borrowed a pick-up truck and we drove into the country to cut and gather drying grass from the side of the road – hay for our animals during the coming winter. By evening we had built a huge haystack in the bed of the truck. Frankie and I rode home on top.

We were riding high. We didn't know about hard times.

CALIFORNIA BOUND

"There's nothing for us here," Daddy said one day. "The crops won't grow. There are no jobs. Your brother, Elmer, says to come to California."

"Up and leave? Everything? Our house? Our friends? Our church? What will we do with Ma?" Mama asked.

"We'll bring her with us. What chance do the kids have in a place like this?"

After much agonizing they decided to make the move. My brother, George and I would stay and wait with Gramma until Mama and Daddy found work. Nanny, the brown goat, would come to Gramma's, too.

"My girl is always sickly," Daddy had remarked to his cronies.

"There's a fellow over to Eureka, what has a nanny goat come fresh," one of the men had said. "Take my pick-up truck and go get her. They'll let you have her cheap. Goat's milk is good for them that's ailing."

The milk tasted terrible. The Hershey's chocolate syrup that Mama added was the envy of my friends. All the girls drank goat's milk when I served "tea" in my China dishes.

Now Nanny would be sold. Everything was sorted and packed – some to sell, some to ship later.

"You may pick two toys to take to California," Mama said.

"Only two?"

Mama relented when she saw the tears in my eyes as I tried to choose between a box of paper dolls and a toy sewing machine that really worked.

"Put the rest of your toys in this box," she said. "Maybe the renters will let us store them in the attic till we can send for them."

I packed more than toys into the attic. I packed my childhood. The new pink wallpaper Mama had pasted over the studs in my upstairs room. Long hours twisting and spinning on the tire swing. Peggy, my friend and tormentor, the golden Persian cat who spread herself across the paper dolls I had arranged on the floor or stole the snack of cold creamed peas I had saved from lunch. Plus Mama's garden, the smiling yellow house with the perfect Andy-I-Over roof and yard, the hole George and I were digging to China.

We children were frightened and excited at the thought of moving. We barely blinked to say good-bye as we moved our clothes to Gramma's. Mama and Daddy caught a ride with someone going west. We couldn't fathom 1800 miles. We only knew our folks would not be coming back.

We felt secure with Gramma. Nanny gave us milk. Fresh shoots of green asparagus appeared on stalks like magic every other day. Gramma baked bread.

"Look how the Lord provides," Gramma said when the three remaining hens each laid a daily egg.

Gramma still lived in the upstairs flat of her converted home. A family with two boys lived below. Raymond was my age and in my class at school. I never played with him. He was a boy and I was shy. The outside stairs led to the kitchen. Once it had been Uncle Elmer's room.

Gramma clucked incessantly, "The renters are ruining my oakwood floor." It had been her pride. She had always kept it glistening gold. Grampa had laid it years ago, long before Haley's Comet, when Mama was a girl of ten. I loved to hear Mama tell that tale.

"It was a clear cold winter's night when I was but a girl. Pa came in from closing up the barn. 'I've asked some of the boys in for a game of cards tonight," he said. Ma never blinked an eye. Just went straight into the kitchen and started making sandwiches and cake.

When the men had played some rounds one of them said, 'Say, Will. Do you reckon we can see that comet yet?'

"May as well give it a try," he answered.

They pushed their chairs away from the table and shuffled out the side door, through the screened-in porch. I followed close behind, said Mama – though your Gramma never once looked out. The stars were bright and blinking and our footsteps made a crunching noise on the hard packed snow.

There before us in the sky spread the comet, with its long, majestic tail. It was so awesome!

'Well, Will,' one of the men said to Pa. 'Next time it comes around, we'll all of us be gone.'

'They forgot about me,' said Mama."

I began to have an aching feeling in my stomach – missing our parents. California seemed even more remote than Haley's Comet.

"Let her come and spend the night with us," Aunt Dorothy said to Gramma. "It'll get her mind off being lonesome."

She helped me choose a dress from the Sears Roebuck catalog. "You'll need something new when you start school in California."

It was a perfect choice – for a little girl. I didn't wear it long. I would be twelve by Christmas.

When I got back to Gramma's there was a letter from Mama. "Your dad has gotten work at a dairy farm. He's not used to milking and his fingers are all puffed and swollen and they hurt. But at least it is a job. Uncle Elmer found a house to rent, big enough for all of us. Some people that he knows give me a job working in their cafe."

"What will we do?" I asked Gramma. "We'll have no furniture. Without our beds, we'll have to stand up in the corner to sleep."

Gramma laughed and shook her head. "Ja, ja. I'm sure they'll think of something. Go on. What else does your mother say?"

"Uncle Elmer took us to the World's Fair in San Francisco," I continued. "The picture I'm enclosing was taken there. As soon as we can make arrangements for a ride for you, we'll let you know. School will be starting soon. We miss you. Love, Mama."

I stared at the picture. "Mama has a new dress and coat. Do you think she'll know me when we come?"

"Ja, ja," Gramma said, tapping me softly on the head.

That's really Mama, I thought as I looked at the picture again. Mama didn't look a bit like Gramma. Gramma was fair and round and had a jolly face. I loved to pinch her fat cheeks and jiggle them. Mama was olive skinned and had a hawk-like nose. People often asked if she was Indian. Maybe the spirits from that Indian grave in the corner of our property had cast a spell on her. She loved to ride her pony and commune with animals.

I thought of myself as plain. Some said my eyes were green. Some said that they were hazel. I figured that meant motley. Gordon must have liked my pigtails for he dipped them in the ink well once at school. He was too funny to stay angry at for long. His humor earned me D's in Deportment until Mrs. Stieger moved me to the front. But Keith was my hero. It would be hard to leave him behind.

Soon after, we received another letter saying that a Mr. Evans would come by on August 23rd to pick us up. He covered his expenses to California by taking riders. Gramma arranged to have the trunk and boxes shipped. We each carried one small case – plus Gramma's shopping bag – filled with cans of orange juice, homemade bread and sweet rolls, fried chicken, and plenty of oatmeal cookies.

"I thought you told my daughter there'd be six people. I count seven," Gramma said when she saw the crowded Chevrolet. At least it was four-door.

"I got this extra rider," Mr. Evans answered. "The girl is little – she can squeeze in."

There was nothing Gramma could do. No matter where I sat – in the front or in the back – I made the fourth one in the seat. Gramma's treats were welcome relief. We rarely stopped. The miles and miles of flat prairie land seemed endless.

"Look there, girl," Mr. Evans said, pointing to the grass. "That looks kind of like the ocean. Wait'll you see that!"

I had seen Big Stone Lake ripple in the wind like this grass. "They should call this Prairie Lake," I said.

"Yeah. I guess," he answered, looking back at me through the clouded rear view mirror.

I was afraid of Mr. Evans. He seldom talked to me – it made me feel embarrassed.

Before long the Bad Lands – where horse thieves once hid from sheriffs and posses – were left far behind. Left behind, too, were the Black Hills where Buffalo Bill Cody and General

Custer had entered history. On and on we drove. Two and a half days – non-stop except for gas and rest rooms. It felt more like a week.

"I thought mountains were pointy and had snow on top," I said as we wound through the tree lined passes. The misty dawn crept beneath tall pines, snowballing the darkness in its path. Pictures never looked like this.

"This is where the Donner party camped," said Mr. Evans.

"Who are they?" I whispered to Gramma.

"Some pioneers who froze to death one winter."

I looked at the blue lake and green trees. It seemed impossible. A cold shiver went up and down my spine and I snuggled close to Gramma.

"What are those funny little plants? Are they the walnut trees?" I asked when we came down into a valley on the west side of the Sierras.

Mr. Evans looked out across the fields and grinned. "Those aren't trees. They're grape vines. That's what you call a vineyard."

I felt myself go warm and vowed to save my questions for my parents.

"Sit still," Gramma said. The trip was wearing on her patience, too.

"Come on," said Mr. Evans. "You can climb up in the front and get a view of your new home town."

As we crested one more hill the road curved into a tiny valley, green with heavy laden walnut trees and ripening pears. A little town nestled in the center.

"This is where we live?" I asked in awe.

"This is it," said Mr. Evans. "Walnut Creek. It shouldn't take us long to find the house. The place isn't all that big. We should be in Lodi before dark," he said to the other passengers.

"They said Locust Street runs parallel to Main. Yup. Here it is," – thinking aloud as he drove through town.

He pulled up in front of an old but friendly looking house. There was a porch across the front and a steep slope to the roof. Three large walnut trees grew in the swale.

I was so excited I thought my heart would stop. Mama had told us the door would be unlocked. (It was the usual thing). When we got inside I stopped still. Not one piece of furniture or knick-knack looked familiar. Is Mr. Evans right? Are we really in my parent's house? Opposite the front door a stairway led upstairs. I ran up the steps and peered into the rooms looking for a piece of home. There atop a built-in chest in a cozy knotty pine room, stood pictures of our family.

"This is it," I called down to Gramma. "We're home! I found them on the dresser."

TORN FROM PLACE

The place was right again, but only for the moment. The soil of my garden had been potted and transplanted. Strange, exotic flowers in the new land led me to compare them with my prairie blooms. I heard talk of Okies – people driven from their homes in search of jobs. Okie. An epithet spouted disdainfully by my California classmates. Daddy came here hoping to find work. Does that make me an Okie, too? Doubts crept in about my worth. I tried to hide my background. I tried to hide the essence of my pollen. I mustn't let them know – I felt – more than I thought.

Brave enough at first to raise my hand and speak in class, I curled back into my bud when they laughed because I said "awnt" instead of "ant" for aunt – like I'd learned in school. Quiet by nature, I sat back and watched, taking note of differences, assimilating nuances of sound and style, gleaning information dropped in casual conversation. Trying to change my image, I wrapped my long, thin braids in crowns and coils on my head. And watched.

I felt a oneness with the Gypsy girl who camped by the railroad tracks. So different from anyone I had ever known. Skin the color of a hazelnut and long, black hair – plied and intertwined. Yet it was her eyes that drew. Haunted hollows, filled with tears long dried, echoing the sorrow of two people torn from place.

I felt a sense of gratitude for Cindy – a girl who lived nearby and was hungry for a friend. We both went home from school for lunch. Cindy to the soda fountain where her mother worked and I home to Gramma: thick slabs of homemade bread filled with ham and cheese, a glass of cold milk, and quiet time together across a faded oilcloth on a well-worn table.

"Cher- ISE. Cher - ISE!" Cindy called before we were half way finished eating.

"That dumb girl," Gramma clucked as I hurried out. "She don't let you eat in peace.

But it didn't pay to affront her. Friends were scarce in this new flowerbed, especially since the dance. "You shouldn't dance with boys," Cindy warned. I wondered why. I had been glad when Keith asked me to dance in my Dakota world. Perhaps things were different here. Something deep inside told me to be careful. So, when Steve, the secret love of all the girls, asked me for a dance, I demurred. I might have become the belle of the class. Instead, I became an enigma. The boys stopped asking me.

A few tried sending secret notes for me to meet them at the movies. But Cindy's influence was powerful. If I tried to be assertive, she tortured me with tickles until I acquiesced.

Cindy was not in my room at school. There were times when I was free from her directives. Like the class outing to the San Francisco World's Fair. Mama packed a brown bag lunch – something new for me. A yellow school bus drove us halfway across the Bay Bridge to Goat Island, then down to Treasure Island beside it. I was overwhelmed walking through huge halls filled with exhibits of agriculture and geography or watching historic drama-ramas and Esther Williams with her ballet water maids. It was better than the Diamond Jubilee back in Dakota.

Mr. Fox was our teacher. He had spent time in Argentina and was eager to share his experiences. No more books and tablets. We would learn by doing – the modern way. He put part of the class to work building a hut in the corner of the classroom. Others painted a jungle mural across the wide side wall. He sent a few, including me, out beneath the pines to create a play about gauchos and bolas, for the class to perform. Buddy pecked on a portable typewriter while the rest of us fed him lines. Later, the class became more serious and studied journalism. We made a field trip into town to the Oakland Enquirer and watched how the experts produced a daily paper. Back in our classroom we were eager to start a paper of our own. It seemed I had learned good grammar in my "Okie" land. Once again Mr. Fox chose me to write.

After school I was back in Cindy's sway. Her parents often invited me to go places with them to keep Cindy company. On Sunday afternoons they liked to go to San Francisco to visit

Cindy's Uncle Mike. The drive through the hills (where I saw my first real deer) to the long curving tunnel into Oakland, was treat enough – topped by the long approach to the toll plaza, where we stopped to pay a quarter, then up and over the Bay Bridge. Its silver spans looked like graceful necks on giant swans – floating high above the waters of the bay.

Uncle Mike owned a tiny corner store on Geary Boulevard, halfway to the beach. It was dark and dank and cramped. He and Cindy's parents sat around a wobbly table in the back – behind a curtained doorway. They placed their coffee mugs on the crackled oilcloth and laced them with a shot of whiskey. A gloomy place for kids. Uncle Mike took pity on us and went into the store. He clanged the till drawer open and took out some dollar bills – plus some streetcar change. "Go on out to Playland and have yourselves some fun."

Any kid would think they'd just been sent to heaven. Not me. Scary rides were torture. The ferris wheel at the Diamond Jubilee had been bad enough for me. But Cindy was bold. She doled out the money and let me choose the easy rides first. We spent time in the fun house listening to The Fat Lady laugh and laughing at ourselves for looking fat in The Hall of Mirrors.

About the time I thought I was home free, Cindy would announce, "It's my turn to pick now: the boat slide or the roller coaster?"

I *never* chose the roller coaster. Please, God. Don't let Uncle Mike give us any money; I prayed the next time an invitation came around. Answered prayers come in unexpected ways. Cindy's dad was transferred. I was free again. Free and frightened. I needed Cindy yet. But Cindy was gone.

LAZY DAYS

Like a tulip bulb, lying dormant in the earth until spring, I waited out my summer of transition between the security of grammar school and the beginning of high school. Soon after school vacation started, Mama's brother died. His wife and son, Aunt Flo and Cousin Don, came to live with our family until they could get established. Although younger and pesky, Don satisfied my need for friendship. I had the know-how now, and he the need to learn.

I took him down the tree-lined street to Fixit Jones' yard, on the corner of Locust and Diablo. What started as a repair shop in Fixit's garage had overflowed and blossomed into a giant junkyard with things people brought to be fixed and never came again to claim. Things he kept because he loved them: old wheels and clocks and toasters, radios and bikes, pieces of iron, rusty garden rakes and mowers and long bamboo poles. Don liked to fix things, too. He stood and gaped across the fence.

"Come on," I called. "You gotta see the grammar school. It's got a million steps."

We crossed the busy intersection, passed The Legion Hall, and climbed the street to the foot of a high knoll where the schoolhouse stood. Don ran ahead and flung himself across the playground bars.

"Come on," I called. "You gotta see the steps."

"Where they at?" he asked, jumping off the far end of the bars.

"This way – to the back."

"Is *this* what you call a million steps?" Don asked as we came around to a short flight of stairs leading to a side door.

"Huh uh. It's down around the side."

"Wow!" Don cried when he saw the dusty, needle-strewn stairs that lay beneath tall pines. "It's like a park."

And it *was* like something we had never seen on our prairie plains. We scrambled down, coming out from the wooded schoolyard slope onto South Main Street, past Elks Hall – much in need of paint – and headed north toward home.

"We got a letter from Aunt Dorothy today," Mama said. "Your cousin, Joyce, is coming for a visit."

And so my summer without Cindy, never did hang heavy. It was a time for sleeping late and walking to the library. Trying to decide which book to read Joyce and I took turns twirling around with our eyes closed. The book we pointed at when we stopped was the one we were supposed to take. But "How to Build a Rabbit Hutch," sent us into peals of laughter until the librarian threatened to oust us. Home again with a series of "Ann Porter, Nurse," we settled on the sofa and began to read.

When Joyce went home, I realized with a shock that summer was almost over. I spent the two remaining weeks with Cindy in the valley town of Woodland where she had moved. I returned to find ten library books – overdue two weeks. It used up my whole allowance.

I might as well go back to school, I thought. The prospect of high school frightened me and intrigued me as well. George was there. He had survived the change. And I had fooled these kids so far. I had proved I was no Okie. Life was a strain. But what the heck. Here I was. I cut my braids, wrapped them in white tissue paper, and laid my girlhood in the drawer.

WAR TORN

I'm fourteen years old and my brother *still* hasn't come home from the war – World War II. U. S. Infantry, Private First Class. If a girl ever needs a brother it's in her teens. This war's followed me all the way through high school. So far. I'm a sophomore now.

George was here my first year, keeping his eye on me like the time I met him in the hall during class with his friend Swede.

"What're ya doing out of class?"

I had my permission slip in hand but never thought to ask what he's doing. Swede had a car. They were off to someplace fun!

I bet Mama never knew he did stuff like that. She sees no fault. You should've seen her expression that day George and Swede came running up our front porch. George asking did he get his? You know – draft notice. Mama didn't like it – not one little bit. She always used to say she wished she could take us far away from war. Like to the South Sea Islands – until we started fighting there. That's Mama's way – always trying to save us from something: poor health, fires, anything bad. Always blowing out the candles before we barely smell them or stuffing us with vitamins.

But she couldn't keep George from war. She does what she can though – writing air letters, sending packages. Cookies, chocolate bars, warm socks – for when his feet get cold and wet in a fox hole. European theater you know.

I try to do my part, too. Scrounging around for foil from cigarette packs and Wrigley's chewing gum wrappers and rolling it in a ball. Mama uses our ration books carefully. She's always worried we don't get enough meat. You know – protein. So she started raising rabbits. That's a laugh. She gives most of them away. Can't bear to kill 'em. Dad can't do it either. But that's not really war like in the news reels or the movies. The movies aren't really war either. Our side always wins. Like in the "Flying Tigers."

So I've been going along making do without a brother. Well – that's not exactly true. When Uncle Walter died Aunt Flo and cousin Don came to live with us. He's been kind of like a brother – only younger and pesky. Not like George. When my cousin Joyce came for a visit we got so tired of him we took our library books and climbed up in the neighbor's tree to read. It's a big ole fig tree – so thick with leaves he couldn't see us. He'd call and call. We just kept on reading until our legs got tired being so scrunched up. Then we'd get down climb up the back porch and sneak into my bedroom through the window. We'd stretch out on the bunk beds (knotty pine) and read some more till he came by and asked where we'd been. What d'ya mean? Been here all the time.

That porch is good for sneaking out too. I wish you could see the roses climbing there in spring. American Beauties. Really red. I always pick a big bouquet for Mama for Mother's Day. She took a picture of me standing by them in my confirmation dress. I felt pretty grown-up. Still – I like to play hide and seek around the funeral parlor. It's scary after dark. I guess a grown-up wouldn't do that.

I say the country may be in war but that doesn't stop the walnuts from growing. We have these three big English walnut trees in front and one black walnut in back. Actually they're all black walnut to start and then they graft the English ones onto the stronger trunks – something like that. We never use the black ones much. They're so hard to open and you have to be a lawyer to get the meat out (That's what Mama says). Come September Dad gets the bamboo pole out of the cellar. I love the musty smell down there. (Not the rats.) The walnuts are covered with a thick green husk. When Dad knocks them down it looks just like green rain. The hulls crack open when they hit the sidewalk – hopefully. I say hopefully because then us kids have to carry them to the backyard by the bucketful and tear the hulls off. If they haven't split by falling you have to use a knife. I hate knives. Then we spread the wet walnuts on pages from the Sunday paper and leave them there to dry. It's an icky job because the sap oozes onto your fingers and turns them brown.

You have to scrub for days before it comes off. Everyone at school knows who's got walnut trees. George's off risking his life for us and here I am worrying about brown fingers. And everyone else in town is celebrating walnuts. Well – the town *is* called Walnut Creek! Every year after the harvest we have this big festival. There's a carnival and parade and all. The mayor and other politicians ride in their convertibles and wave. The ranchers ride their horses. All dressed up in fancy riding clothes. Silver buckles jingling spurs cowboy hats whatever. The ladies wear bright colored ruffled skirts and embroidered peasant blouses. Like at a square dance.

Don went to the carnival with me last time. He tried to talk me into going on the airplane ride but when I saw it spin and turn upside down I was out of there.

Afterwards we went to the Elk's Club barbeque and stuffed ourselves on ribs and corn. Did you hear?, he says. Mr. Bruebaker's palomino won first place in the parade. I was glad. Mr. Bruebaker's always nice to me. He owns the auto shop on Main and our house is kitty corner across the alley from its back door. He never gets mad when we short-cut through. He's in charge of the school buses and when it's real stormy he lets me off right at my front door. He gave me a job filing receipts and bills once a week in his office.

Walnuts aren't the only things that need harvesting around here. The farm workers went off to work in the shipyards and factories but tomatoes can't wait for peace. So us kids get commandeered on the work crew from school. We change into our gym shorts and get shuttled to the fields in big open-bodied trucks. Twenty-five cents a lug working in the hot sun and adobe dust. The smell of fermenting fruit and droning from the buzzing bees puts you in a kind of trance and sets your insides roiling, especially working close with boys like that. They keep looking at your legs. We stash away the biggest ripest tomatoes for our ride back and get rid of those feelings throwing red beef steaks between the two trucks. A kind of war within a war, but fun. Seems like everything I do for the war turns out fun, except going without my brother. One day I came home from school and found this really cute sailor visiting with Grandma (Mama was at work in the walnut sheds). This is Jimmy says Grandma. A friend of your cousin back in Dakota.

He's stationed here in Alameda. Blond – blue eyed. I tried to still the rattle in my heart – lolled back on the sofa listening to them talk. Grandma poked me. Sit up! Why do grown-ups always read something into everything we do? (Maybe she was right. I did feel seductive.)

Mama wouldn't let me go out alone with a grown-up sailor but Don chaperoned. Good for something at last! Jimmy and I never even once held hands but you don't need to touch – to feel. It just comes sizzling through your arms like one of those electric wires left dangling from a storm Mama always warns us about. He's out to sea now but I liked being with Jimmy. He comes from South Dakota like me and is used to things like our old cracked paint house and second hand unmatched furniture. He gave me status with my girlfriends too.

A few weeks ago Marion, a Catholic, invited me to a dance put on by St. Mary's to entertain the soldiers. These guys were on their own – not like going to the Sophomore Hop with Dewey and being chauffeured by his parents. (That's not putting Dewey down. He's sort of round and not very tall but I like the way he makes me laugh.)

The dance was just the same though; same agony looking at that wide room waiting to be filled. Will someone ask me to dance? Same strains of "Sentimental Journey" coming from the record player. Only this was big time stuff with soldiers. They seemed like men to us. We weren't much to look at with our bobby socks and washboard chests. They liked us anyway. Home girls. Fresh from church. Trying to warm a soldier's heart with smiles. No matter that our sweaters sagged. Then I had to go and spoil it. I'm a prince from Hawaii. Will you dance with me? he says. Of course I would. You remind me of Calinda – back home. I didn't like to be like someone else but it seemed a compliment. How could I rise to that image? Me – a plain girl from a poor family. We wear uniforms to school I say. Some girls are poor and can't afford expensive clothes. We get around that by the sweaters we wear. (A monster lie. I hate myself.)

War is everywhere. Nothing brought that home plainer than that Western Union Wire: "We regret to inform you, your son George has been wounded in action." Mama almost fainted. When it finally hit her that he wasn't dead she was relieved.

Until the word "wounded" grew pictures in her mind – some unbearable. She was almost glad when we finally found out it was something he can live with. At least he won't have to go back into battle.

George told me how it happened. It was the night before the famous Battle of the Bulge. Their battalion was scheduled to cross the bridge in the morning. His platoon swiped a couple chickens from a Belgian farmer and settled in his house. They sat around the pot-bellied stove waiting for their meal to cook. One of the guys fiddled with his grenade and pulled the pin by accident. George was the lucky one – holed up behind the stove – the only one alive. His wrist and hand were battered and he lost half his right index finger. My cousin told me later that our other Grandma back in Dakota got everybody up that night and made them pray for George. She always did have ESP.

I didn't know I could ever be so glad when we heard George was transferred from the hospital in England to one in Los Angeles. Mama had to see him. Dad had to stay home and work. So she and I set off for the Greyhound Bus Depot in Oakland.

At first it felt like we were in a church with that big dome and benches shaped like pews. Then I saw the dirt and scruffy people trying to catch a ride somewhere – like us. Bus #27 to Los Angeles now loading at Gate #2 blared from a speaker. I swear it felt like we were pulled along with the crowd. Like undertow at Santa Cruz. We were way far back. The bus was filling up fast. My heart sank. We'll never get on!

Then I got this vision. Dad shoving his way to the front of a ticket line making sure we wouldn't miss our one chance to see the Ringling Brothers Circus. I snatched our tickets out of Mama's hand slithered through the crush and waved them underneath the driver's eyes.

"We gotta see my wounded brother."

"Let her through," the driver says. He closed the door behind us and we hunted out the last two vacant seats.

"MISS H."

Miss Hamburger, my English teacher at Acalanes Union High School in Lafayette, California, during the 1940's, was affectionately called, Miss "H" by her students. We girls loved her most for her role as leader of the extra curricular activity modern dance (a la Elizabeth Duncan).

A lovely woman, with striking black hair and a lithe slender body, she taught us how to move ours gracefully, to hear stories and see movements in music, to create and choreograph. We gained self-confidence through her acceptance and encouragement as we performed before an audience at spring and fall concerts. Our appreciation of music grew as we danced to "Hungarian Rhapsody No. 2," "Go Down Moses," or Tchaikovsky's, "Sleeping Beauty Waltz." Dance brought aspects of our subconscious out from behind our ego masks and let them move and be exposed.

But it was in her English class that I learned the most valuable lesson she offered. "I'm going to read you an article on anti-Semitism," she said to the class one day. "Then I want you to write a paper discussing it." I had never heard that term before and didn't have a clue as to what it meant. The article spoke of Hitler's aggrandizement of blond, blue-eyed Aryans above other races; of pogroms, ghettos, and discrimination involving Jews. I had been brought up in a Christian setting, sent to Sunday school and studied Bible stories. To me the word Jew simply meant God's people in the Old Testament times. Why should they be treated badly?

That day, seated in a wooden desk in a small classroom, my eyes were opened to the horror of racism. My innocent world of family, friends, music, and dance was suddenly expanded to include sounds of suffering from people outside my little circle. I strongly defended the Jews in my essay.

Just as dance brought out my feelings, Miss "H"s' introduction to prejudice was a stepping-stone to inclusiveness. Her lesson, assimilated at a formative age, helped me deal with relationships in creative ways. Ultimately, I gained an international family: an African-American son-in-law, a Mexican-American son-in-law, a Jewish daughter-in-law, and even an Episcopalian (I was brought up Lutheran). Miss "H" wove patterns of tolerance into my life, allowing me to celebrate and appreciate the variety in my expanding family.

PAPER MOON

"Eat the crust," Grandma said as I reached around it, to a soft white piece below. "It's good for you."

"You eat it then!"

"Sassy girl! Wait till you're hungry. You'll sing another tune."

I was sixteen – summer of '45. More interested in boys than in Grandma's advice. I pushed my plate toward her and headed toward the bathroom. Frowning at myself in the mirror, I daubed make-up on two red pimples erupting on my cheek.

Who'll dance with me like this? (thinking of our impending trip). *No more chocolate till we go.* Jan and Lisa went every summer. A family type place where Highway 120, heading for Yosemite, makes a hairpin turn across the Tuolumne River. It was the last summer before we graduated from high school. For a special treat, the girls' parents agreed to let them stay on longer this year. Marion and I were invited to join them. Jan told us that boys from Berkeley Camp often came by the lodge – evenings after chow. Mama wasn't sure she should let me go. Grandma was quite certain it would lead to no good. I saved my money from ushering at the local movie theater – determined.

We boarded the Greyhound bus, heading for adventure – boring at first through the valley towns. Gradually we began to climb the summer gold hills, peppered with green live oaks. Small streams trickled through the hollows. The road got steeper and more twisty. Sparse stands of pine appeared

Jan and Lisa met us in the parking lot, fronting the cafe. Their parents had left that morning – back to the Bay Area for work. The girls had kept one of the apartments: two bedrooms, a kitchenette, and living area. A girl's dream: sleeping late, swimming in the river, sun bathing on large grey rocks beside the rushing stream with quiet time to read or nap, supper in the café, ping pong in the rec room, jukebox music dancing with the boys from Berkeley Camp. No parental guidance.

Pimples gone – Rob developed a crush on me. Letting him win at ping-pong was no trauma. With my double-jointed elbow I never could throw straight. But I could dance. And loved it.

"Paper Moon," playing on the jukebox. Swaying to the rhythm. His arm about my waist . . .

"You go to Berkeley High?" I asked, my head against his shoulder.

"Yeah. What about you?"

"Acalanes. Out in Lafayette."

"Not so far. Maybe I could come see you." I smiled.

Rob and the boys came back each night with coins for the jukebox and Nehis. The week was rushing by faster than the river far below. Wednesday already. That night, abandoned by the boys' race to meet camp curfew, a full moon blossomed above us.

"Let's go for a walk," says Lisa.

"Where? We might get lost." Me – Grandma style.

"Along the railroad track. Can't miss that." Our paper moon glowing overhead, we picked up the tempo with, "I've been workin' on the railroad," sung in loud raucous tones.

Thursday came with an invitation to join some of the boys Friday night – into town and uncertain territory.

"You think we really should?" Me again. Friday came and so did Rob – set to spend the afternoon and evening. I packed my beach bag and we slipped away. Down the river to a large hunk of granite. Flat enough for tanning.

We dipped into the water, rubbed sun tan lotion on each other, lay on our backs talking. Turning on my tummy, I leaned on my elbows and began browsing through a copy of *Seventeen*. Looking up I caught Rob peeking down the front of my bathing suit and felt my insides melt. He pulled me close and kissed me.

"Dance with me tonight?"

"We saw that!" teased Jan.

The spell was broken. A big to-do back at the lodge – who was going to town – who would ride with whom. Rob and I waved them off – settling for a burger and fries out on the deck, a rousing game of ping pong, dancing. Dancing close and dreamy. Feeling body things. Things I'd never felt before. Warm. Exciting. Alive. A lingering kiss good-bye. The promise of his letter, "Soon as I get home."

I lay awake – dizzy from the evening's new feelings – worried for my friends. Until I heard cars squeal around the bend and stop. Doors slam. Laughter. Loud voices.

Back! Happy. Unscathed. With local gossip about "those rowdy city girls at the river lodge, singing long past midnight, loud and drunk, eyes glazed, high."

"High? On Nehi?"

After a good laugh and rehash of our evening, we fell asleep. No need to get up early. The bus wouldn't come till afternoon.

Along about lunchtime we straggled up and began packing our bags. No more time for swimming or ping pong. No more money for a snack at the cafe. No more food in our cupboards. Nothing but two hard crusts in the bottom of a bread bag. Feeling starved, I broke them in half and shared them with the others. We went out front and climbed aboard the bus. Home to a letter that never came.

SHORELINE

I was seventeen. A senior in high school. A bit younger than the others. (Started school at five). My cousin Don and his mother invited me to go with them to visit Aunt Flo's brother. There's nothing like spring in California. The almond trees were blooming that morning. Feather blossom white. Carpets of yellow mustard spread at the feet of pear trees lined in meticulous rows. Hills - covered in green so new - looked chartreuse. Orange poppies and purple lupine spread across the slopes. I was ready for a ride.

My mother had recently bought me a new coat. Light tan with dark toned flecks of tweed. Quite grown-up. The day was sunny. Cold enough to wear my coat. We drove north to the Carqueniz Bridge where headwaters of the Sacramento River spill into the Pacific Ocean at Benecia Bay. Once across the bridge, we angled back along the shore - a narrow strip between tall cliffs and bay. The houses were anchored at the edge - extending into the water on stilts: a paradise for fishermen with boats. The tide was out when we arrived. Soft gray-brown sandy muck reflected the sagging sun. The grown-ups settled in with talk.

"We're going for a walk," Don called to them.

He headed toward the bridge. I followed - in my brand new coat.

"We'd better not stay out too long," I stewed. "The tide might come in and trap us."

"There's lots of time."

Rounding a corner, we came upon an abandoned ship beached atilt above us.

Look at *that*! Let's go explore." Don started toward it.

Fear swept over me. Fear without images. Telling me to stay away. I kept walking forward - fast - trying to lead him from that deserted hulk emanating DANGER. In my desire to escape, I jumped down onto a flat patch near the shore ahead. Immediately I began to sink. Quick sand!

Don clambered down the bank and pulled me out. He led me back to his uncle's place – bedraggled and mud-soaked. Aunt Flo took one look and shoved me in the shower. New grown-up coat and all.

No matter that she treated me like a little child. A Hand had reached to save us from impending danger on that derrick ship. I felt safe now. And dry. I listened to the sound of chicken, frying in the kitchen and the water lapping beneath the stilted floor.

Listen . Cherise, Listen. There is more ....

DECISION TIME

Robin, the boy next door, and I were sitting on the hood of Daddy's car talking and enjoying the warm evening. As we peered up, trying to find Orion, the sky burst forth in a shower of myriads of stars.

"What's happening? I cried – frightened as usual.

I ran into the house calling, "Mama. Come outside and look. The sky is falling. Is it the end of the world?"

But Mama only came and said that it was beautiful and wasn't it past time to come inside and go to bed.

"Pretty soon," I said. "I'm going to wait and see if Jesus comes."

A few moments later I was sure it was the Second Coming. First a brilliant flash, then the houses shook and rattled with an earthquake force. Everyone in the neighborhood ran outside.

"Must'a been at least a five on the Richter," Robin said.

"Part of the ceiling fell on top of our bed," said the man across the street. "Good thing we weren't in it."

"I thought Dad was playing games with me when the table jerked," Mama said, as she wrapped her arms in her apron trying to ease her chill.

Robin's Dad came running from their house pulling on his naval officer's jacket. "It wasn't an earthquake," he said. "I just got a call from Port Chicago. The ammunition ship I'm stationed on blew up. I have to get there right away."

Everyone stood still in shock and gaped at him. It had been his evening off. Aunt Flo worked at the base as a payroll clerk and often had to work late. Today they had finished early. Uncle Elmer and Daddy worked there, too, on a survey crew. Years before Daddy had fallen on some rain slick steps and fractured his skull, losing his sense of smell. But even *he* could smell the stench of decaying flesh when the workers were allowed back in the area.

The horror of war, so vividly exposed, unsettled Daddy's stoic nature. War was hell, even to the ones just partially involved. We *had* to get it over with. He would vote for Roosevelt, fourth term, no matter what his friends decided. Not so, Uncle Elmer.

"We've never had a president three terms before, let alone four," he protested. "We're no better off than Germany. Roosevelt's nothing but a durned dictator."

When election-day arrived, Mama invited Elmer and Elsie for supper and to listen to the returns.

"Well? Did you vote for Roosevelt?" Elmer asked as he cut his pork chop.

"Of course," Daddy answered with a sly grin.

Mama nodded yes and Gramma gave a weak, "Uh-huh."

Then everybody looked at Elsie.

"Well?" Uncle Elmer replied, staring combatively

"Yes," she answered meekly, looking more mashed than the potatoes on her plate.

"You did *what?*" Elmer shouted. "You mean you cancelled out my vote? What kind of wife are you?" They went home soon after. I never heard the answer.

One day my dance classmates and I were staying late at school for a rehearsal when someone came into the gym and said, "Roosevelt is dead."

"So are Washington and Lincoln," I quipped.

"I'm not kidding. It's on the radio."

Everyone gathered close to listen as Miss "H" turned hers on. The air waves were filled with news of Roosevelt and Truman, history interlocking future, tuned to the waltz of a Missouri music man. It was the beginning of the end of war and the end of my new beginning.

Decisions had to be made about the future. Should they involve that blonde, curly headed boy who had spent his life in India as a missionary's son? Or what about that tall good looking guy whose parents socialized with Mama and Daddy? I had met them both at church and that was good, for my parents and the church strongly recommended I marry someone of my faith.

Both of these boys seemed ready and willing to attend the youth group meetings at church in spite of the long trip from their boarding school in Oakland. And they were back in Walnut Creek for the Sunday evening worship service at the Women's Club where a group of Concord's members was establishing a sister congregation.

After the service the ladies served refreshments. The teenagers had clean-up duty. That's how I met Mart. His uncle brought him into the kitchen one night and introduced him to us.

"This is my nephew, Mart." he said. "He's here with his parents who are on furlough from the mission field in India."

"Hi," I said, looking up from the dishpan in the sink. I reached for a tea towel and handed it to Mart. "Here," I said. "You can help."

Mart became a faithful member, even taking on the job of playing the piano for the services. I helped with Sunday school. On Christmas Eve Mart's parents came, too, and saw me lead my little group in their performance.

"That's the girl for you," Pop whispered to Mart. "Set your sights on her."

He already had. But I wasn't settled yet about how to spend my life. I liked being around boys. I liked the idea of closeness that marriage would provide. And Daddy always said girls don't have to go to college. It's their place to get married and raise kids.

But I wanted to study and learn. My friends were making plans to go to the University of California in Berkeley. Some were being rushed for sororities. I had taken the proper courses and had the grades, thanks to Uncle Elmer's direction. Going into Berkeley and finding their way through the campus seemed second nature to my friends whose parents paved the way. I had passed the Subject A test and was accepted to enroll. But I was scared. I agonized until registration day, (a word, along with rushing, I barely understood). I could visualize boarding the Greyhound bus. Beyond that loomed a black hole.

"I don't feel well," I called to Mama from my upstairs room. "I don't think I'll go."

Mama didn't mind. In fact she seemed relieved. Perhaps she had glimpsed that black hole, too.

"Stay home and rest a while," she said. "Take time to get your bearings."

The church had taught me not to waste my talents. One should choose a calling, honorable and helpful to others. Reading through the official magazine of my church, I saw an ad for a summer course at the prep school in Chicago. Enrollment in parochial schools was growing, not so much from a sudden interest in religion, but because "Johnny couldn't read." Church schools still taught phonics and the regular 3R's, plus the fourth, religion. The summer course was being offered as preparation for emergency teachers to fill the sudden lack.

How to get to Chicago? Daddy wouldn't send me to college, even if he could afford it I would get a job and earn my own way.

"HOW WAY LEADS ONTO WAY"
... Robert Frost

"Why do you want to do that – go to Chicago?" asked Mart, who still had a year at the Oakland Prep school where he was studying for the ministry.

"I'm not going yet," I answered. "I got a job in Oakland working as a route clerk for Western Union. I should have enough money saved by summer to pay for the course and get there."

It was an easy job in the traffic office, taking wires off the end of a belt and routing them to the proper dispatcher. I often found one that was addressed to me, one of the guys, asking me to meet him after work. But more and more it was Mart I found waiting. He seemed lost with his family back in India, yet he seemed to know his way around. He took me to restaurants on Broadway and bought me dinner from his hard earned cash, something the other fellows never did. He always had a job or two. After meeting me, he found one at a service station in Walnut Creek. Then there were funerals and weddings where he earned extra money playing the organ or piano. He was a go-getter, that was evident. And determined. He had set his sights on me and would not let me go.

"Promise me you'll write when you get to Chicago. And don't forget. You're my steady girl," he said when it came time for me to leave.

I was confused. I wasn't sure what steady meant. How long did steady last before it became permanent? How binding was it anyway? But I couldn't sit around and wait to see. For now, I would serve the Lord by teaching little children. Daddy shook his head in disbelief.

"I left my home in South Dakota and brought you here so you could get an education and find opportunities for work. Now you shrug it all off and go back there to school."

Education? I mused as I began to pack. *I thought he said girls should get married and raise kids.*

Daddy did not give his blessing. He watched me fold my dresses and lay them in the trunk and worried for his little girl. And Daddy had a point. Earlier I had lost my nerve trying to find my way fifteen miles into Berkeley. Now, here I was going 2,000 miles or more to one of the country's largest cities. How was I going to find my way from Union Station to the college? I had never even sat inside a taxi, let alone hire one to take me clear across town. Then I remembered Jesus' words to seek the kingdom of God first and the other things will be added to you. I felt my goal was right. I was determined now to go. My seat assignment on the train put me next to an older woman. I was used to older women from my years with Gramma. It was second nature to open the door and hold it for her or listen to her talk. When the woman realized how frightened I was of finding my way to the campus, she put my mind at rest.

"Don't you worry anymore," she said emphatically. "My son plans to meet me with his car. I'll see to it that he takes you out to River Forest to the college."

And so I was transported from my doorstep at home to the front steps of the school. I was assigned to a room with a dozen other girls, most of whom were my age. I settled into dorm life and grew bolder as the group ventured on the El, visiting museums or climbing the dunes on the shores of Lake Michigan. The quiet plop, plop, of the wavelets gave me a sense of peace, but when a handsome fellow from school asked me for a date, my heart surged more like the wild waves of my familiar Pacific.

"What did you tell him?" asked Lenore.

"I told him, 'Thank you for the invitation, but I have a steady beau at home.'"

"You said what?" cried Fran, one of the older girls. "Life just isn't fair. I go to sleep every night wishing for a boyfriend and you turn extra ones away."

Fran threw herself onto her bunk and turned her head to the wall. I looked at the other girls and shrugged. But I never forgot Fran's despair. Perhaps Mart was not someone I should take lightly. He surely showed he cared.

The summer experience left me brave enough to find my way on a hard-benched train from Chicago to Dakota to my aunt and uncle's home in the southern part of the state. They drove me north to my old home town to visit Gramma. When I left, Aunt Lizbet packed a picnic bag and put me on the train through Montana, Idaho, and Washington. In Seattle I caught another train home to California. Join the church and see the world!

After my return I got a letter from a school in Southern California, looking for a teacher for grades 3-5. Just what I wanted. But when I spoke to the superintendent on the phone, he said he preferred that I teach grades 6-8. Who was I to argue? When I arrived in Los Angeles I found someone who could.

"*You?* Teach those big lugs? You're nothing but a kid yourself," roared Mr. Harris, the chairman of the School Board.

Although I didn't like his attitude I was happy with the outcome – assigned to grades 3-5 – 42 faces. Ellen, the 1st and 2nd grade teacher and I, roomed and boarded with Mrs. Thompson, a widow lady from the church. Mrs. T. babied us and fixed us brown bag lunches, washed our clothes, and gave us sumptuous suppers. It kept me going as I struggled every night, studying the text books, trying to keep one step ahead of the kids. Correcting workbooks and homework had to be squeezed in. Mart helped me out more than once when he hitch hiked down to visit me on weekends. His granddad lived nearby in Inglewood. Mart took me there to meet him. I fell in love with the old man at once. I now saw Mart in another light. He belonged somewhere, not just a lost school kid. He didn't seem to mind that I was a South Dakota Okie. I felt free and strong with him. I felt myself being pulled by a force I could not name. I was not ready yet for marriage, but I knew I could not let Mart go.

So it was, when he came down to watch my class perform on Christmas Eve, I finally said yes to one of his many proposals of marriage. We took the midnight plane to San Francisco for Christmas and told the family. When I returned from the holiday, I was sporting a diamond ring on my left hand. I would have lots of time to teach. Mart still had to finish at the Seminary.

But Mart had never really felt a call to the ministry. His dad had urged that course of study because Mart had no other plans. Now with our engagement, he had himself a goal. He would finish the school year. Then he would get a job.

I was committed now to him now and returned home when school was out, not renewing my teaching contract. But Daddy wouldn't let me get married until Mart found a decent job. Toward fall he got one in a bank in downtown Oakland.

It was a happy wedding. The new Walnut Creek congregation had built a parish hall in which they now held services. Mart and I were the first ones to get married there. Everybody came and brought beautiful useful gifts. I felt like a princess and Mart my handsome prince. The place was right again.

Thirty five years later, I found myself thinking of enrolling in some classes – another university in another strange place. The black hole loomed again. This time I ignored it. I had seen how way leads onto way.

THE PREGNANT CAMPER

It was 1950. I was twenty-one years old and pregnant. My brother, George, had returned from World War II minus half a finger and with a strong wanderlust. He led an erratic life – taking surveying jobs in places like Alaska and Mexico or looking for lost gold mines in the Superstition Mountains. My husband, his brother Larry, and I often went with him on his treks.

George had been a good shot as a private first class so decided to take up hunting. He got himself a rifle and invited us to go someplace with him over Labor Day weekend to try it out. We scrutinized maps of northern California until we found a place to camp far from civilization – Meadow Lake, north of Donner Summit. We packed our camping gear and set out – me bursting my jeans with the baby due in December.

The long winding dirt road through the mountains and down to the lake was well worth the trouble. It sparkled clear and clean, surrounded by a wide sandy shore. We began setting up camp close to the lake. Behind us the trees grew thick on the rising slopes. No one else was there. I took a deep breath of the scented air and felt the blissful silence away from city noise and fumes.

We had hardly begun pounding in the tent pegs when my brother spotted a deer. Without a thought, he grabbed his gun.

Come on," he called to Mart as he dashed up the hill in pursuit.

"Don't get lost," I called.

"We'll fire a couple shots if we do."

Then they were gone.

What good is that going to do? I wondered. I busied myself setting up the cooking supplies and equipment. Larry finished the tent job and filled the pots with water from the lake – our only source for drinking – after boiling.

It was already far into the day and it would soon be dark. Silence settled on us now like a heavy drape.

What if something happens with the baby and I need a doctor? It's a long ways out of here. I didn't know how to drive and began to fret. I guess Larry could drive me if it came to that, I consoled myself – until I realized – we didn't have the keys to the car. They were in my brother's pocket.

"What if they <u>do</u> get lost?" I worried aloud.

"Let's gather some wood for a bonfire on the beach. If they aren't back by dark, we can light it and guide them." Larry was worried, too.

We scuttled around stacking branches and twigs until we had a tower – taller than myself. The sun had set behind the Sierras when we heard the shots.

Here! Here we are," we called desperately – over and over again – until we saw two sheepish men return to camp.

"You left us here without the car keys," I remonstrated. "What if my labor pains had started?"

"I'm sorry, Sis. It *was* a stupid thing to do," said George. "We followed the deer up the hill and immediately lost track of him. By then we were lost, too. We wandered around and around, till we finally found a road."

"Come see our wood pile," Larry said. "We were going to burn it and help you find your way back."

"Neat," my brother said. "Let's make it higher."

As we worked a ranger drove up, eyeing our stack.

"You're not intending to burn that, are you?" he asked.

We explained why we had built it and in the end he relented. "The lake is low and the beach is wide. It should be safe. Go ahead and light it."

And what a sight that was. Bright orange flames reaching for the night sky – snapping and crackling. Making a song. Darkness – where people can get lost – was all around us. The fire drew us near in a circle of warmth and illuminated our togetherness. Brother, brother-in-law, husband, baby and me – safe.

FIRST BORN

"I think I'm pregnant," I said to my husband.

Skipped periods, blossoming breasts, and a general feeling of activity bursting inside me had left little doubt. Married in November, it was now well into June of the next year. There was no such thing as birth control pills. I probably wouldn't have used them anyway. We were young and poor and happy.

My husband had just been promoted from gophering cokes to the bookkeepers in a local bank, to their "Pick-Up" department: a service, which brought the bank to the customer via a driver and a van – a kind of teller on wheels. One of his weekly routes took him to Pill Hill – a hilly part of Oakland where many doctors and hospitals were located.

"There's a nice old doctor I pick up from," Mart said. "I'll make an appointment for you next time I'm at his office."

It wasn't until my husband got sick and I called Dr. Bell (white haired, kind, and gentle), that I found out he was a gynecologist. Even when they politely informed me, I was so naïve, I had to ask what that meant. So here I was not only feeling pregnant, but very embarrassed.

And here I was with this body that sometimes walked on air and at others left me curled in bed, nursing nausea. My friends often teased me about my hearty appetite, saying my middle name was "Hungry." Now it became my first. An illusive feeling to satisfy, as food now made me sick – a constant battle between my desire for food and my repulsion of it. Crackers and a cup of hot tea at my morning bedside (recommended by Dr. Bell and served by my husband) got me through the worst.

Eventually the feeling of elation won out over nausea and I bounced around like a Mexican jumping bean with something alive inside – twice alive. I could feel my nipples swell from pokey peaks to soft-sloped hills. Next came the sense that I was toting a heavy back pack on my stomach – setting me off balance, making me feel awkward and old like Gramma, when I tried to get up from a chair. I felt young and expectant, too – on the doorsill of a new adventure and fulfillment.

As the months moved on, images of babies born blind or without an arm or kidney, began filling my mind with worry words. Would my baby be whole and healthy? Would I fall apart if it weren't – or would I cope?

And what about the pain? At the time, obstetricians were just beginning to turn to natural childbirth techniques. Dr. Bell didn't offer to participate from his position, but he gave me books to read on the subject. I remembered the horrible feeling of losing control when I'd been given ether during an appendectomy, and wanted no part of that. I was determined to be awake to greet my first-born. But I was frightened. Would I be able to bear it?

All speculations and worries stopped a bit before midnight December 12th when my water broke. Contractions two minutes apart immediately, sent us scurrying for a taxi to Merritt Hospital on Pill Hill. The pulling in my middle back felt like what I'd imagined people experienced when they were placed on a wrack. Pull and tug. Pull and tug. Then release and a little rest. But the contractions were coming so fast there was little relief, so they gave me a shot to slow them down. Pull and tug. Pull and tug. Then one small whiff of chloroform and a final push. Our son was born.

The red-headed OB nurse, with a reputation for gruff commands, held him over me to see. My first impulse was to reach up and touch his little feet dangling above me. With a quick jerk, she pulled him back. "You can't touch him yet." Off she went to clean him.

Can't touch him? I carried him around inside for nine months – now I can't touch him?

But I had let him go from that warm place into another's hands. My first inkling that he wasn't *only* mine to hold – there were and would be others.

STIR-FRIED GENES

"Man will never reach the moon," my father said. A man of old traditions – faith. Clearly man was reconstructing Babel's Tower reaching into space.

Change is never easy. Perhaps one of the hardest challenges in America, is to love our neighbors as ourselves – in spite of physical differences. Civil rights, put into action.

Change of sorts was molded in my father's bones. It had started with his parents, a young couple from the Steppes of Russia, seeking opportunity in America. His mother's mother fainted on the dock when she came to wave goodbye. This farewell was final. The depth of her bleak sorrow was mirrored in the blackness of her dress and the babushka pulled tight across her brow. Eyes burned deep despair. There was no "Reach out and Touch Someone" in the late 1800's.

The couple settled on a homestead in the prairies of Dakota. From farmer, to merchant, to preacher (in between the circuit rider's visits), postmaster, and proprietor of the town's hotel – Dad's father ran the gamut. "Change" became Dad's middle name.

He became a farmer, like his father, but his career was halted by the draught. For a while he claimed a new one, as town marshal. When that was over he decided to move us out to California. A whole new life at forty: job, friends, church, surroundings. How he missed the flatness of the prairie where a sea of grass spread to the rising and the setting sun. Hills and mountains, thick orchards, dense with walnut trees, penned him in and made him wonder if he'd done right to change?

So when it came to grandkids, he had been schooled for change. First it was my brother's kids: second-hand by marriage, fresh from Tijuana, Mexico. Dad couldn't understand a word they said, but they learned quickly to say Poppy, gum, and candy. A crying baby needs a cuddled-rock in any language. In no time he was claimed as Grandpa. He learned to eat tamales.

My oldest children ushered in the hippie age: patches on the jeans; long hair; strings of beads made of acorns, buttons, twists of metal, sandals. Next came Diana's boy friend from the heart of China Town. Chop-sticks were the in thing Jeanine's black husband was welcomed. Dad's door was open to them all. "Just don't forget to come and see me," is all he ever asked. It threw him for a loop though, when they landed on the moon. Even so, his faith in God and man survived and he kept on praying "Thank You Lord," when he sat down at his table, surrounded by people of mixed races and religions.

"My family," he would say with pride, "my international family." It had been a long, long journey from babushkas and the Steppes of Russia. A kind of giant step – like Armstrong's on the moon.

MANIFEST

How can I tell this tale that took so much time and touch? Say what needs be said. Say I miss him. Say I can't abide his death. Why can't I cry? I who loved him so.

Such was he – a man who believed in God. He carried whiffs of God, strong as the scent of cheap cigars that lingered on his clothes. He was my husband's Pop. I owned him for my friend.

A child prodigy. They bought him an upright Stein. He played upon the stage at seven and could have been a concert pianist But his heart was elsewhere than the stage and fame. One could say his heart had one beat in heaven.

Already a bit different from his Los Angeles school friends, he batted piano keys in lieu of balls. Son of a man's man: soldier in the Spanish American War, engineer for the Santa Fe – weeks spent in the California desert, directing men who lay the tracks. As the son of this man, Pop was no sissy. Yet his heart had one beat in heaven.

It was people that Pop loved – and beyond their earthy selves – their souls.

There was nothing of this earth he loved better than plain people. And so instead of symphonies and stage, he headed for the seminary. In route he fell in love with the lovely Paula. Such was his love for people, God, and souls, he kept the college rules – abstained and put off marriage until he graduated.

Now at last he claims the dark-eyed Paula. Now they sail to India. People, people, people. There are people everywhere in India. They press upon you as you walk. They sleep in doorways inset from the street. They make their homes beneath the rising ramp of road exposed to passersby. They bathe in ponds with oxen and there they wash their clothes. And they all have souls.

Twenty five years, a career, spent in South India speaking, joking, laughing, loving, giving whiffs of God through care. Touching plain humanity, not fame. Bartering with merchants in the market. Walking snake infested jungle trails to villages. Sacrificing family for souls: Mom and Dad experienced alone through mail – letters and magazines; children sent to boarding school at the tender age of six; a wife who might prefer a faucet to a well, a tidy bathroom sans a midnight snake. All for people and their souls. How great a love appears sometimes in a humble human man.

Health problems bring him back to the U.S.A. It was here I learned to know and love him. It was here he became my friend. Two kids, another on the way when they arrived, he and his lovely Paula and their school age kids. Always ready for a game, cranky kids were turned to laughing elves; boring dinner parties into deep discussions lasting longer than the candles that matched the room's decor. He was a helping hand that reached the tender spots: sweeping up the crumbs from dinner, rescuing a broken clothesline draped with heavy sheets, listening to my theories. His was a hand that touched plain people issuing warmth and healing.

How the people of his parish loved him. Too much perhaps – though he never asked for adoration. He only cared for people and their souls. How fitting it should happen in the Easter season. A season surely meant for souls.

The Sunday after Easter. A visit after church. I took his face into my hands and kissed him as we said Good-bye. It was our last Good-bye. How I loved this man. How is it I can't cry?

Why did he find it necessary to fix the church's plumbing? Rise that morning, dig down to the pipes? Why did death's toll strike? Perhaps because one beat of heart already was in heaven. Perhaps the leaven of his life sufficed. Perhaps it is symbolic that such a man, fit for fame, spending life on souls, should die digging ditches to repair a sewer.

He was my friend, my best friend ever. Why is it I can't cry? Is it because I know his earthly beat is joined to the one in heaven? And yet I wonder why.

Time passes. My husband and I are vacationing on the island of Grenada. It is the end of fall, a time for the Advent of the King. Plain black people dance and party late into the night.

Early morning finds them gathered on the beach singing, "Hark The Herald Angels Sing." Their music drifts now through my dreams along the sandy shore. He stands before me there, mingling with plain people singing, "Hark the Herald Angels." And at last I cry.

PERSPECTIVES

Imagine a teacher having not one – but two – of her own kids in her classroom. That's me. Grades three through five. Forty kids. Bethlehem Lutheran School, Berkeley, CA. Early 1960's. The middle grade teacher resigned shortly before the fall term began. I offered to help out if they couldn't find a replacement. Naturally they stopped looking. They seemed more concerned about finding someone with the right religious background than my lack of a teaching degree.

Bethlehem is an inner city church school. The building is Spanish style – pumpkin pink – roofed with red tiles. The original plans to dig out a social hall next to the church and build a large school on top, had to be halted due to lack of funds. After the basement was completed it was divided into three classrooms with sufficient space left for socializing. A cold cement stairwell leads down from Prince Street. The fenced-in playground looks like a prison yard. But the neighborhood blacks are anxious to enroll their children here – a school that actually teaches kids to read.

My classroom has high windows that peek above the ground level onto the parsonage garden. The room is furnished with old-fashioned wooden desks with hinged tops and seats. So here my girls are stuck with their "old" mother in this old fashioned classroom.

Diana – third grade. Jeanine – fifth. They don't know what to call me. Mostly just plain, Mama. At least it's not Mr. Nitz like some of them do– after the man who just resigned. Others call me, Teacher – in an affectionate sort of way.

"Teacher, do I have to drink my milk?"
"Teacher, Danny hit me."
"Teacher, will you play with us at recess?"
But my girls are not happy having me as Teacher.

"There's entirely too much noise in here," I say one day. "I want you all to sit straight in your seats and put your feet together flat on the floor." A pause.

"There. That's better. Please continue reading Daryl. Bottom of page five."

"He never was quite sure what time it was. He couldn't remember if two o'clock was before seven o'clock or after five," Daryl continued.

SQUEAK! SQUEAK!

I looked around and found Diana, last desk- first row, blithely tilting up and down on the edge of her metal-hinged seat.

"Didn't you hear me, Diana? I specifically asked you all to sit straight in your seats. That creaking is disturbing." Daryl continued reading.

SQUEAK! SQUEAK!

Annoyed, and keeping my place in the book as Daryl read, I moved to the back of the room. I gave my daughter a tap on her bottom and sat her down with a firm hand.

"Now stay put!" The other kids laughed. Diana looked around and blushed.

* * *

I'm in the third grade at Bethlehem. My sister, Jeanine, is in the fifth. Our mother is the teacher. Ugh! At Mandy's school they have nice new metal desks with arms. We have these old fashioned wooden things with people's names carved in and a hole that's called an inkwell. (We never even use ink.) But the seats are neat. They move up and down. I like the sound it makes. Mama doesn't like it. I guess when people get old – they can't stand a lot of noise.

I sit way in back of row one – as far away from Mama I can get. It's enough being under her thumb at home. Today she found me out. I was doing my spelling work book (I really love spelling) and I happened to tilt the seat up and sit on top of it. I made a kind of rhythm with the words and squeak. And then – you know what Mama did? She came storming back to me and spanked me hard. And scolded me – right there in front of everyone. They all laughed.

***

"Mama spanked me hard in school today," Diana told her dad at dinner. "Just 'cause I'm her kid."

"You probably deserved it," he replied – helping himself to another slice of meatloaf.

"It was just a little tap," I defended myself.

It was hard on all of us. But a united perspective came at last – the day President Kennedy came to town. The entire enrollment walked the two short blocks to Shattuck Avenue to watch his entourage pass by. We waved and called when we spotted him and he returned our greetings.

"We really saw him." "We saw the President." "Right On!"

Not long after, the president was assassinated. Yet a tiny piece of him remains – deposited for life in eighty-seven memory banks. Teacher's included.

DEAR DOCTOR

Dear Doctor is a letter that I imagined my mother wrote. It entails experiences I heard her tell about and embodies a picture of her loving character and acceptance of what life brought her. It keeps her alive in my heart and allows her to still speak wisdom to others.

Dear Doctor,

It was good to see you today and hear you say I've got at least 50,000 miles left on me. But when you reached to shake my hand – somehow I knew just what that meant. He's retiring.
How can you do this to me – after all we've been through together? You're still a young man. You've got so much to give yet. What are your fifty years compared to my ninety-three?
Forgive an old woman's presumption in offering her opinion. It's just my way of saying how much you mean to me – how much I appreciate the kindness and care you've given me and my late husband, Joe.
Oh, I know that's a sore subject with you. You always blamed yourself for insisting it was better to let the sleeping cancer lie dormant than to roil it up by trying to cut it away. But you did what you thought best. What more can anyone do? Who can know which way was right? We never blamed you for it. My husband thought the world of you.
And all that business with your wife – in the news and all. It must have been terribly disturbing to you. Yet you kept right on seeing to your patient's needs. That's the kind of thing people notice – not how many degrees are plastered on your wall – or if your belt matches your shoes. Like that time I had my appendix out and my granddaughter brought me a bouquet of sweet peas. I can still see you bending over them and sniffing

their sweet scent. It's things like that, that make a person real. And when you're sick in bed you want someone real taking care of you. Not some robot in a white coat.

And that time after Joe had his radiation. The treatments did reduce the tumor in his esophagus, but in the meantime he'd not been eating much and was sinking fast. Then his friend from the pool hall came to see him and said, "Hey, Joe. How'd you like a nice cold beer?"

"Sounds good to me," Joe said.

"Give it to him," you said. "Anything to get him eating again."

I know alcohol is against your religion and all, so I'm doubly grateful for that extra year you gave me with Joe. I figure it was the beer that gave him back his appetite.

When I came to see you about a year after Joe died, I could hardly believe it when you asked me if I was still sleeping on the sofa – like I told you I was doing when he was first gone. How did you remember such a thing? And after all that, when I started losing my sight, you sympathized and helped me find my way around. I can still hear you tell your nurse – the one I liked so much – "Help her. See to it she finds her friend in the waiting room."

Oh, Doctor. I can't tell you how much that meant to me. You seemed to understand how frightened I could feel, not seeing where I was. It's an awful thing – going blind in one's old age. It happened too late for me to catch on to reading Braille. I kept thinking I would die soon and it wouldn't matter. Yet here I am with your predicated 50,000 miles left. Except for these arthritic knees, I'm in the best of health. But what's going to happen now when I get that bronchial cough next winter? Will the new doctor know what to give me?

And that brings up another subject. You gave me a list of doctors' names to choose from, but said you couldn't tell me which one you would recommend. So I chose the one on top – a woman. (I figured that's why you put her there.) I never had a woman doctor, though I might have liked one early on, when I was birthing my children. What I'm trying to say is, will she understand an old lady's problems? She never lived through them like you have with me.

And I think how much I always wished you'd be there to hold my hand when it's time for me to go. Then I tell myself, "Hey, old lady. Isn't it wonderful that young women are able to become doctors now?"

Then in the darkness of my blindness I see light. I think, Isn't it just like you to give me such a gift – a purpose in my old age – to help a young woman understand old age and help us all to grow.

Thank you Doctor, for everything.

Your patient and your friend,

Lydia

PRIME TIME

I like the phrase, prime time. Its bold, long "I" sounds attract – draw me to examine the meaning. From the dictionary I find that prime – as it relates to time – refers to the peak hours when most viewers watch TV or listeners tune into the radio. A time most profitable for advertisers. A time that comes but once a day.

When I think of the expression, I get a picture of people sitting in front of a TV set enjoying their favorite show. More specifically I see my husband and four kids watching Wyatt Earp or Ponderosa on a Saturday night years ago. The kids' faces are scrubbed red, hair squeaky clean. Their pajamas smell ironed. With the image comes the feeling of being left out. And yes – I am missing from the scene.

"I never get to watch," I hear myself complain.

Why not? Where am I? I'm in the laundry room ironing a shirt or polishing four pairs of shoes for Sunday school tomorrow. Doing my duty. Leaving myself out.

"Don't worry, Mom," Nick, our oldest pipes up – eyes still on the screen. "When you get old you can live in my back porch and watch all the old re-runs."

His comment was a sop. Someone cared. A portent, too, foreshadowing what life could be like – alone on a porch with no prime people. But it wasn't the sit-com I was missing out on. It was "time" spent with my family purely for enjoyment. An obsession with letting duty override prime time opportunities with loved ones. A sort of knee jerk reaction to following orders – automatically raising my hand when a speaker asks questions like, "How many of you have ever been to Niagara Falls?" Did I come that way pre-packaged? Or was I programmed and by who? A scene from childhood shows how deeply and how early "doing what I am told" was engrained in me.

A boring summer day – lolling around outside Phyllis Holmes' house with the neighborhood kids. After plucking honeysuckle blossoms from her vine along the fence, we nipped off the ends and sucked the sweet honey. Then we gathered in her open garage – my brother, Phyllis, Jackie, Frankie, and I.

"My dad won a big case at the courthouse yesterday," Jackie bragged. "I'm going to be a lawyer, too – or a preacher. Something with class."

I stood back in awe.

"What'll we do now?" someone asked – looking to Jackie.

"Let's have a wedding. I can practice being a preacher."

He looked around at our gang – then pointed to Phyllis and my brother

"Not me," says my brother. "I'm <u>never</u> getting married.

Phyllis blushed.

Jackie turned to us little kids.

Me? Marry Frankie? Live with <u>him</u> forever?

Jackie took one look at my hesitation and grabbed me by the arm. He placed me side by side with Frankie, pulled up a rusty flower stand, took an old Sears Roebuck catalog from a shelf, and opened it like a Bible on a lectern.

"Do you take Cherise to be your wedded wife?" he intoned. "Do you take Frankie to be your wedded husband – till death do you part?"

Barely getting the "I do" out, I left my wedded husband and fled home. Home to my mother's assurance – "God won't hold you to a promise made in play."

Few things in life are as prime as picking one's mate. Of course I was just a kid, but imagine being so attuned to following the voice of authority, that I risked marrying someone I would never choose.

A sheep dog barking out orders to its flock, the church held me in its power with its lists of dos and don'ts. Social niceties – like Grandma's insistence that you must serve more food than your guests could possibly eat (or shoes should be polished for church) – insinuated themselves into the saved documents of my duty file. A default setting, "Love God above all things and your neighbor as yourself," was the first thing to pop up on my desktop screen. I tried to be some person that I intellectualized – living by the rulebook not the heart. Somewhere along the way the "as yourself" got deleted.

Like my visits back to California after we moved to Florida. Three of our grown children had remained in the San Francisco Bay Area. My aging mother lived in the nearby suburb of Walnut Creek. I missed my mother. I missed my children even more. Missed their young adult years and all that entails – heartbreaks, babies, sweethearts. But when I went to visit, I felt it was my duty to spend most of my time with my mother. She needed help – getting to the doctor, finding housekeepers, shopping. We had a good time doing those things together, yet I always yearned to be spending more time with my kids.

They would come out to Walnut Creek after work and have dinner with us or I would spend a night with one. Not the same as going to their house and staying – seeing how they lived – having intimate chats. Deferring time spent with my children until my mother didn't need me any longer. Leaving myself out.

Prime time events are not planned duties on our daily list. They happen unexpectedly. One-time shows that include ourselves as well as our neighbors.

I can still see mine – sick and dying – a lone figure sitting on her front porch. She needs a visitor, I'd say to myself as I pulled out of the driveway heading for one of my women's meetings. When I finally took the time to stop – it was too late. She was asleep in a hospital bed – looking too worn out to waken. She died a few days later. The sit-com was over. There would be no re-runs on her porch. Once again my "duties" had prevailed over the task at hand.

Will I ever learn – or should I? An experience one recent Christmas hints at an answer. I walk into the kitchen where the action is. A prime time spot for women at a dinner party. My daughter and her friend – our hostess – are busy chatting, stirring gravy, sipping wine. I stand around un-noticed – then head back to the living room and the other layaways. No one says, "Come back – stay here with us." I am left out. This time not my choice. I am not alone on the back porch, but I am ignored. Is that how my children felt when I put them second place to my imagined duty?

Prime time is very dear. Ad men vie for it with large sums. It's what's showing on the screen: a neighbor who needs you to stay with her till the ambulance arrives; an unexpected call from a lonely friend; an invitation from your dying father to, "Come sit beside me for a while." Something to be grasped and dealt with at the moment.

Years ago, if I'd sat with my family and enjoyed a laugh or two with them, I'd have given us all much more than shiny shoes. "There is no *later*," says Donald Hall.

A MOVING EVENT

You know how it is – things are going along okay. Boring but okay. Then ZAP. Your husband comes home from work and says he's quit his job. You just sit there and look at him. Feelings and thoughts are tumbling around like laundry in the dryer. You lift your glass, take a sip of your gimlet and smile. Smile? What's to smile about? Your world is coming to an end.

You smile again and take another sip (this time it's more like a gulp). All the while you're conjuring up sweet words to say. And smiling.

Jeff is down the hall in his room feeding his tropical fish, listening to the filter gurgle. Diana's downstairs practicing her flute. You're the last one to know how you feel.

Things proceed in the usual manner of job search. Interviews, trips out of town: Montreal, Portland, L.A. White shirts to iron and pack. Comforting words. Prayers.

You go on washing windows, pulling weeds, making arrangements to rent Chocolate House on the Russian River for an extended family reunion. You don't get to stay because Mart has an interview in The City. You have to go back with him and smile. Say nice words. Make sure he's got a clean white shirt. You're existing in some kind of whipped cream frosting level between the layers of a chocolate cake. Until one day some of it begins to ooze out and drip down the side – right in front of your best friend, Charlotte.

You swipe your hand across your brow, flip your bangs (an unconscious gesture of release?) and say, "I don't know what we're going to do if Mart doesn't find a job he likes soon."

"No point in panicking."

"Can you think of anything worse than being unemployed?"

Charlotte frowns. "You want the whole list or just the abridged version?"

I look past her – into some future – not hearing.

"Aw come on. Cheer up. I'll treat you to a rat burger at the Quick Way."

Our favorite Fast Food haunt for a get-away from household chores and boredom. We stand in line. Watch another steady customer rummage through the waste.

"See what I mean," (nudging Charlotte). "Unemployed."

One day a call comes through offering Mart a top position in a bank in Ft. Lauderdale, Florida.

* * *

"I'm really surprised at Diana's reaction." I take a sip of my Scotch on the rocks. (By now I'm into something stronger.)

Mart sets his on the table between our facing blue upholstered chairs. Stokes the burning logs. "I won't have to do this much longer. I don't suppose they have fireplaces in South Florida."

"I'll miss that." I stare deep into the fire. Warmth stifles a shiver. "Kids are strange. I expected Jeff to be the one to object to the move. It'll be the pits for him – changing schools halfway through his Junior year."

Mart sits down. "He'll live through it." Raises his glass. "Cheers."

"Diana actually cried! Pure and simple. No theatrics. Really, Honey. She is disturbed."

"It's been nothing but 'I want to live in the dorm,' since she started college. Now she has the chance she turns the table and acts wounded. To heck with it. I've got to make a living. Right now that seems to be in Florida."

"I know. It's just that it's hard. Hard to see them unhappy."

With a strong rap, Mart knocks the ashes from his pipe into the blue lead glass ashtray. The smell of roasting pork mingles with tobacco and wood. A buzzing sound from the kitchen.

"Timer! Dinner's ready."

* * *

The job settled – days go fast. My parents are devastated at the thought of us moving so far away. So is Charlotte. Jeanine, our married daughter, takes it hard, too.

I think even our cool hippie, Nick, will miss us being here. No place to come and wash his clothes. At least he's clean. No use in crying over all that again. Better make my plans for the move.

I look out the window from the dining room where I hung Tweetie Bird's cage after giving him a bath. Tall California laurel and live oak entwine their limbs above the creek. It spills into a waterfall below – where Indians once camped. Dried hydrangea blooms give a hint of blue and pink. A few shoots of poison oak expose themselves in coats of red on the western slope.

How I'll miss this place. It must break Mart's heart – after all the work he did on the lower level.

Visions of my new life pass before me – set on a private horror story stage. After Mart's first trip to Florida the bank brought me there, too, to look things over. We were wined and dined. Put up in the Galt Ocean Hotel (one of the best in town). Right on the beach. Dwarfed by a mile long strip of tall concrete condos. Long dresses were "in" for evening wear. Mrs. Tropical, I donned my yellow flowered sleeveless (the one I brought from Jamaica) and the yellow starfish earrings. Took my first step onto the rung of a ladder – to be taken over and over again. Never getting beyond introductions, handshakes, polite questionings. How do you like Florida? Isn't it similar to California? Do you have any kids? I tried to say nice things. Felt my smile mold into a rigid shape.

* * *

The jangle of the phone breaks my reverie. Jeanine. "Hi, Mom. What day is Dad taking off? Is there time for us to have a get together – just our family?"

"I guess so. He's leaving Saturday."

"Great. Keep Friday free for us. We're going to take you out to dinner."

"That sounds nice." *And final!*

Moving plans keep me from dwelling on my fears. Charlotte offers to help.

"I won't have you or the girls to help me in Florida. How will I ever make it on my own? I'm not cut out for that social-climbing set."

"You'll do fine."

"Can't you just see me falling on the tennis court – or spilling tea on some dowager's white carpet?"

That thought sets us off laughing. "Let's go have our drink," I say.

There's a bar on the corner of Piedmont and Pleasant Valley – with a neat stained glass window on the side. It's on our list of things to do. Go in and have a dry martini. Not the kind of thing we ever did – but it was on our list. Time was running out.

Late afternoon. The bar is lined with guys giving us that "What've we got here?" look.

We settle into a booth. Western sun sparkling our stain glassed grins.

"Things could be worse you know," I say.

"Worse than what?"

"Spilling tea on a white carpet."

Charlotte looks at me. A question mark.

"You know – women."

"That could happen anywhere. Why fuss now?"

I stare at my drink. Stir it with the olive. Mart'll be down there all alone till I can sell the house. It may be a long time. You know how men are. Mart is horny as heck."

"You've got a point."

"Besides. When he was down there looking things over he drove one of the gals down to the Keys. Said she needed a ride to see her parents. Went fishing with her dad. Nice and cozy like."

"Did he catch anything?" Charlotte loves to fish.

"Barracuda – he says. More likely she shark." I flick the drips off my olive and pop it in my mouth. "If he wants another woman I wish he'd say so. Before I go through all this work."

"And you say Diana's dramatic?"

"Last night, when he said good-by to my folks, Mama told him not to let one of those Southern belles 'Y'all' him into

59

doing something 'You all' will be sorry for. You should've seen the look on his face! (As if the thought had crossed his mind.) That lying grin."

"What'd you expect? A list of names and addresses?"

"Whose side are you on?"

"You could always stay here and apply for a job at the topless bar. I hear the tips are good."

I wad up my napkin and throw it at her. Reach for my purse. "Time to go."

* * *

Mart might as well be gone, I think as we ready for dinner Friday night. His mind's in Florida already.

"Shall I wear a fancy dress?"

"Aren't I worth it? Hard telling when I'll see you again - dressed or undressed. It may take a long time before you can sell this place."

"Don't say that!"

"You know how long it took to sell our other house. You've got to be prepared. Come on now. Don't fret." He takes my chin in his hands. "Brighten up."

"Here come the others," Diana calls from the hall below.

I blink back my tears and try to sound cheerful.

* * *

A lovely night. This gang could never be glum for long. Not with each one trying to out do the other with their wise cracks. They chose one of San Francisco's Japanese restaurants. Sitting on the floor around the low table makes us feel intimate.

Tears are put away. Sake brought out. Strictly speaking Jeff isn't old enough. Mart coaxes the kimono-clad waitress into bringing him a cup. When he spills his rice she quickly grabs his Sake. "I bring tea. I bring tea."

"Don't be going native on us now, Dad. You know - checkered pants and white shoes." Nick's concession (wearing a sport jacket on top his hippie clothes) puts him in the exalted position of handing out advice.

"Ted and I talked it over," Jeanine says. "Jeff can stay with us till the semester break – if Mom sells the house before then."

He gives her a grateful look. "How about till graduation? Can Blondie stay, too?" (Blondie's his bass viol).

Diana lifts her cup. "Here's to Dad and his new job. Will we ever see him again?!" True Diana melodrama.

Afterwards – it's past old St. Paulus Church on the corner of Gough and Eddy, up the bridge ramp where the smell of coffee always permeates the air, across the bay to home. Lingering by the fire. Taking pictures. Reminiscing. Stalling our good-byes. At last the others have to leave.

Wake me up when Dad leaves," said Diana.

And so when morning came we climbed the stairs and watched him settle in the car amid his boxes filed with pots and pans, blankets, and his clothes.

"Good-bye. Good-bye," we called after long embraces.

"Good-bye. Good-bye," we waved till the car turned out of sight.

"There goes Dad, off into the sunrise. Will we ever see him again?"

Will we indeed? I wondered. Then we turned and went inside, back to our beds, and cried.

GARAGE SALE

I hated garage sales. I'd already "saved" too many things. Why clutter up my house with someone else's discards? So why did I decide to have one?

Circumstances. My husband had taken a job in south Florida. He left me behind to sell the house, move – and wonder how he was spending his evenings. The sign was on the lawn. Nothing to do but wait. Three of our four semi-grown children would not be moving with us. Lots of "stuff" we didn't need. I'd have a sale, earn some money, cut down on moving expenses. My friend, Charlotte, offered to help.

First on the agenda – a trip to the city hall for a permit. I borrowed several card tables from our church. We began arranging things in categories – kitchen, yard, books, clothing. Marked everything low – so it would walk away. Almost as fast as we worked, my kids would come by and rescue a favorite item. "You can't sell this!"

They were probably right. The Bible printed in Malayalam from their grandfather's missionary stint in Kerala, India was something to keep. And the older one – printed in Leipszig 1796 – from great-grandad's parish days when Lutherans in America preached in German.

The house was built on the down slope of a creek – four stories high in back. The garage was attached at street level. Because of the terrain it had only one entrance. That meant hauling things through the front door, up a flight of stairs to the street, and over to the garage. We had the time. No bites yet on the house.

I set the date and put an ad in the paper. Our house was located in the heart of the hills east of San Francisco. Neighborhood estates offered valuable antiques to prospective buyers at their garage sales. Our address was bait for dealers and buffs. Finding nothing special at my sale they stayed and bought my junk.105 St. James Drive. A narrow curvy street – not suited for parking. It didn't take long, the morning of the sale, for a collision to occur. Police were called. Flares stationed at the corner to warn oncoming traffic.

"Mom's really getting carried away with this sale," Nick said when he approached – till he saw the accident.

The first thing to go was my white wrought iron vanity. It made me feel sad. I loved that piece! Garden tools, half used buckets of paint, washed rollers, and paint specked pans went fast.

A set of plastic budding pots lay on the garden table – marked ten cents. "You really think you're going to sell this trash?" a man sneered. By noon they were gone. Even sold that ugly passé pole lamp with the orange, cone-shaped shades.

"I see you're selling your house," a young man said. "We're looking to buy in this area. We'll give your realtor a call."

There was a lull in customers at the moment. "I'll show it to you now, if you like."

I left the sale in Charlotte's hands and led him and his wife down the steps. The beds weren't made, the kitchen counter was strewn with green-streaked plates left from last night's pesto.

On a high from the excitement of the sale, I remarked with enthusiasm on the improvements we had made. Explained our plans for future projects. Pointed out the creek falling twelve feet in a frothy waterfall. Romanticized stories of Indians who had reportedly made camp here. Told how the creek roared as it tumbled through the culvert during winter rains. About the mother raccoon who, finding her kits playing in the yard, sent them back into their nest with a scold and a sharp cuff. About the owl who watched me sew from his perch in the laurel tree and the blue eggs that nested in the top of the California Laurel tree visible from my kitchen window.

"What kept you?" Charlotte asked. "I've been swamped."

That was Saturday. The sale dwindled. By Sunday afternoon nothing left but a few clothes for Good Will. And the faded sofa couch my son decided he could use.

I no longer hate garage sales. It's the best way I know to sell a house.

CRISIS TO EMANCIPATION

*"If the circumstances are right,
suffering can teach and can lead to rebirth."
Anne Morrow Lindberg.*

"Look, Mom!" My daughter pointed out the kitchen window. "A robin's nest."

Two blue eggs nestled high in the California laurel – four stories up from the creek in the back yard. With eager pleasure we watched Mama bird's daily activity – hoping to get a glimpse of the hatchlings. Mrs. Squirrel was watching, too. Her several forages to the nest were thwarted by our protecting missiles thrown at her from the open window – yells, dish rags, wadded napkins, anything within quick reach. Gone from our post too long one day we returned to find an empty nest.

Soon after that event I found myself in a position similar to Mrs. Robin's eggs. I was removed from my nest by my husband's job change from California to Florida, separated from three of my four fledglings who were trying out their wings. The fourth – a junior in high school – moved with us.

After settling in our new house – life didn't seem quite so vacant as my introduction with dinner parties, dresses, and drinks had indicated. Friends and relatives from home streamed in at first. When visits started dwindling I took to going to MacDonald's for a cup of coffee – just to be near people – hear them laugh and quarrel. Lonely and lost, too, my son would come home for lunch. Having nothing on our minds to speak about other than self-pity, we took to speaking gobble-de-gook and blather – just to hear the sound of our voices.

Trying to build a new nest I gathered twigs and leaves – schemes for building a new life. Not a joiner or game player by nature, I even signed up with the Welcome Wagon Club for bridge lessons. A group of displaced beginners who met to practice. (My desserts were the only thing that scored.) I took a course in shorthand and bookkeeping at a local school. Smelled a whiff of glamour from an acquaintance who suggested I model clothes for women's shops with her. (More restaurants and emptiness.)

After a year and a half, finishing high school, our son went off to the University of Florida in Gainesville. At least he came home for holidays and summer. Eventually the time came for him to return to California to do his graduate work and begin his life as an adult. Like Hurricane David the night of his farewell party, disaster was moving directly and steadily toward me. Those strong winds that had been predicted for so long were close enough to feel and hear. I saw them bend the bushes and heard them crackle through the palm fronds like a raging fire. What will I do with my life now?

I tried my hand at women's groups – League of Women Voters and church committees meetings, programs, phone calls. Talk without relationship. Still a robin's egg torn from my nest.

I began taking my morning coffee to the patio. Heard the wind chimes whisper through the screened in porch of our neighbor's empty house. I felt empty, too. Empty and disconnected – as though a vital wire was missing from my life. My dad used to laugh and say that if he touched an electric fence when he was in the field surveying, he'd get such a jolt he would run up and down those hills all day. Faster than the young guys. I began to see just what he meant. I had to get re-vitalized, too.

Through the years I noticed that letter writing helped me organize my feelings. Why not try putting them on paper now? I began by making two columns – the pros and cons of my situation. The results set me to wondering. Am I in a state of crisis? Or emancipation? A page, called, "Now I Think," in my church periodical, invited readers to express their opinions on current social issues. A popular topic at the time dealt with mid-life crisis. Perhaps a timely subject for the column. The publication of my article was the force that drew the storm away from shore. The carrot that led me to pursue a latent love of writing. I had long held a secret desire to write stories for children. How do I proceed?

Nothing along that line was being offered in the local colleges, so I opted for taking a course on writing poetry. Something I had always loved. A way to start. I signed up, but the class was cancelled. Not enough enrolled. The instructor encouraged our small group to transfer our registration to the Central campus. "Class starts at 8: AM." Too early for me! But then – I'd already paid my fee – and I do enjoy the sunrise. So my first appearance, was the class's second. An assignment had already been given. Scanning my registration paper, Dr. Grande, the professor, quipped – "With a name like that, she doesn't need to write well." An uplift that didn't last long. I now had two assignments to deliver and had missed the introduction. I devoured everything the instructor said or read and soon became hooked. Until the day he began reading our work aloud. Wonderful! Too wonderful. My heart made a fist choking out the flow. I felt it skip a beat and coughed. My insides were on fire. What am I doing here? I could never write like that. It wouldn't be polite to walk out in the middle of the class, but when it's over I'm going to drop the course.

Then Dr. Grande read my poems.

"Don't you wish you could write like this?" he said when he was finished.

They weren't Pulitzer Prize material, but it was a moment that changed my life. One that gave me purpose beyond raising kids – kids who grow up and leave home. One that led to publication of my articles and poems and the thrill of sharing my thoughts with readers. One that led to friendships – people of like mind – writers. One that led to emancipation – a life of my own. Free to fly – be a bird.

MOVING ALONG

"You'll need a whole van," the agent said after he had evaluated the amount of goods we were taking on our long move – California to Florida.

I was not only leaving behind our lovely house built on a steep hillside, but the small creek that flowed through the backyard and fell in a ten foot waterfall. It was hard to give that up. Even harder was saying good-bye to parents, children, relatives, and friends. Three thousand miles would be too far for drop-in visits. Yet, for now, Charlotte was still close by – offering to help any way she could.

Charlotte is a woman tuned to nature. We often took walks together in our neighborhood or long hikes with our children on nearby state park trails. She gifted my life with treasures that she found: colorful leaves, feathers, a rose from her garden.

One day she brought me a stone from the creek bed of her family's summer home, a large, smooth oval-shaped stone that seemed to speak to us. I placed it in the front garden near the cherry tree I'd planted. Whenever I walked past it, I would think of her.

Now all that would soon be over. The van was scheduled to come Friday after Thanksgiving and I made arrangements to fly out that night. My husband had gone ahead to report for his new job. When moving day arrived, Charlotte came to see me through the trauma. The van appeared on time – half full of someone else's goods.

"We'll have to send another truck tomorrow for the rest of it," the driver said.

"I can't wait until tomorrow," I replied frantically. "I have my airplane ticket for tonight."

"Don't worry," Charlotte intervened. "I'll come by tomorrow and take care of everything." A person not only tuned to nature, but also to people's needs.

I was busy unpacking the first load when the second van pulled up at our doorstep in Florida. The last thing to go on and the first thing to come off was my stone. Charlotte had rescued it from the yard. I placed it in the center of our rock garden where it sent warm vibes as I came and went – a symbol of our solid friendship.

After several years in that neighborhood, the people next door adopted a baby. Alex was a sweet child, but somehow always seemed lonely and sad. As he grew, he loved to come across the lawn and play with the stones in our front patio. I would hear him out there, talking to himself contentedly. One day, after he had paid his usual visit to our yard, I found an empty space where my stone had been. The empty space moved to my heart as well – as though I'd lost a friend.

I debated about asking for it back when I felt a strong objection – as though the stone were saying, "It's time for me to move along. Alex needs a friend like Charlotte."

SCATTERED BEADS

The strand of earth-toned beads broke and scattered on the tiled floor. A rust colored one rolled beneath the bed – clear to the other side. Others somewhere in between. One landed in the corner by the closet. Some behind the dresser. An olive green oblong, nestled in the foliage of the oriental runner.

Shades of my life, I thought. Torn from my family – four children, parents, relatives and friends – 3,000 miles away. Now even *he* is gone this weekend. Mother's Day weekend. A time for family and kids.

I moved here with him because of his career. Ft. Lauderdale, FL. A snowbird's paradise. An unreal world of fancy dress charity balls and a silent telephone. No morning chats with Charlotte. No rat burgers at the Quick Way on a fast lunch break together. No lunches with Mom and Dad at the Berkeley pier. No more leaf-crunching walks through the park.

Instead – frantic trips to McDonald's for a cup of brew – served with people. People who talk and laugh and argue. Make sounds. Arduous safaris through Publix Supermarket stalking items packaged in unfamiliar skins. Frustrating drives finding routes through city streets road blocked by canals. Smiling. Always smiling. Cocktail party smiles. Coming up short when someone calls out, "Mom." Dropping down again when I know they can't mean me. Endless beginnings with party people. "Where do you come from?" "Do you like it here?" "Do you have a family?" YES! YES! YES! Beads – scattered here and yon.

Got to get a hold of myself. Where's that clipping from the "*Herald*"? MacBeth playing across the state in Sarasota at the Venetian Theater. Brought across the sea and reassembled there. I'll take a little ride. See the sights. Rent a place on the beach.

I pack a bag. Head west on Alligator Alley through the everglades. A part of Florida that intrigues me. Pa-Hay-Okee –

River of Grass. A wide, wide river of shallow water, barely flowing from Lake Okeechobee in the center of the state. Emptying into the Straights of Florida at Flamingo in the south. A river disguised by saw grass – stretching from horizon to horizon. Their serrated blades, multitudes of mosquitoes, heat-heavy humidity, lurking alligators, craggy lime protrusions and potholes, make me wonder how the Seminoles survived in such a harsh environment.

The birds seem to like it. Egrets, cranes, and ibis feed on bugs or stand stock still, stalking fish in nearby sloughs and roadside canals. Their white feathers adorn trees like blossoms as the western sky bursts in flash bulb brilliance from the setting sun. I'll never tire of this scene.

And now it gives the comfort of a family memory. One son and a daughter with her husband on a visit. A late evening call from our hippie son, hitchhiking down from Massachusetts. "I'm out here at the edge of Naples on Alligator Alley. The guy at the service station says there are gators out there. Can you come and get me?"

I smile – remembering how we filled two thermoses with homemade limeade, stuffed a pack with chips and cookies. Happy hugs on finding that lone figure waiting by the dim station. Then back across the Alley where an army of land crabs was being crunched beneath car wheels as they crossed. A side trip onto a dark road – beyond lights from the Alley traffic – to stop and stretch, listen to bull frogs add tympanic notes to this swampland symphony, watch fire flies flit about, gaze at the sky dropping star-drops thick as snowflakes in a winter storm. A late night lark with lots of laughs. Did we ever go to bed that night?

Yes. I'm glad I came out here today and met this memory.

Naples at last – then north to Sarasota. On time to locate my hotel on Long Key, have a bite to eat, and find the theater. A tour next day of the Ringling Mansion and the Circus Museum. Sunday morning – Mother's Day. Time before checkout for a walk on the beach. Fine white sand so different from the eastern shore. I puddle along – forgetting the time. Am I late? A man approached in my direction. "Can you tell me the time?" A quick reply. A fast retreat – as though my innocent question had been a vamp's proposal.

Lovely scenes, great production, interesting collections – yet without anyone to share them they piled up inside like stones along a graveled path. Not one word exchanged beyond ordering meals or tickets – or my timid man. Silence so heavy I felt it physically – sending feelers of self-pity through my psyche like large rocks, shifting in the earth.

Seated alone at a Denny's counter – waiting for my order – he came and sat beside me. Young. Long, hippie hair, like my son.

"Hi there, Mom," he greeted. "Where's your family today?"

An invitation to join him on the beach. Pleasant talk and smiles that softened the hard stones blocking my throat, and let the food flow through. Scattered beads – restrung.

ONE OF THESE DAYS

"I think we finally got some human beings for neighbors." I was coming in from putting out the garbage.

"What do you mean?" my husband asked.

"I just heard the new people. She was giving him the "what for."

"It figures."

We had lived here now five years and this was our third set of neighbors. After those last weirdoes, normal sounded good.

I must greet them, I told myself.

She beat me to it the next day with a "Hi, I'm Grace," as we met at the curb when the garbage truck had passed.

"Welcome to our neighborhood," I said

Grace nodded toward the large green dumpster. "If you're not here, I'll bring yours in. No point in advertising no one's home."

"Good idea. We'll do the same for you."

Eventually the scales were hopelessly unbalanced. Grace had the duty nine to one. If I was home, I wasn't up on time. If the garbage truck was late I didn't notice. Always occupied. Being president of the church women's organization proved to be more time consuming than I had anticipated. Phone calls took forever. Countless meetings, correspondence, literature to read, planning to be done. I couldn't find the kitchen counter for all the reminders strewn across.

One morning I heard a scraping noise and poked out the side door of our screened in patio. I found Grace – hoeing underneath the key lime tree between our white Floridian houses. "How about a cup of coffee?" she asked. She swiped her hand across her forehead, pulled off her floppy hat, and fanned herself. "I could use a break."

"I better take a rain check. Got to be in Hollywood by ten for a meeting."

She looked disappointed. "How about tomorrow morning?"

Next morning over coffee she told me why they'd moved there. "My husband had to retire early because of an injury. He couldn't take the cold up north. It broke my heart to leave our daughter and her kids."

"I left my kids in California. I know just how you feel."

And so a warm bond formed. We'd wave or share a break occasionally. But it was always me it seemed who had to renege.

"Soon I'll be finished with chairing the women's group. Then I can go to the dog races with you guys. Sounds like fun."

After finishing with the local group I was given the job as chairman of the assembly. It took me even farther afield – to Homestead or Miami.

"One of these days," I'd say. "I'm going to have some time."

"We're going to Bermuda for our 30th Anniversary," I said to Grace one day. "Will you bring in our mail and watch the house?"

"Be happy to. Have a good time."

Bermuda authorities were cutting down on traffic by prohibiting the use of rental cars. Tourists could take a cab or rent a motorbike. We took a taxi tour the first day to get a flavor of the place. Each bend in the winding road revealed a bay – bluer than the one before. The hills reminded me of home – in California.

"Let's retire here," I said. The hillside graveyards fascinated me.

Next day Mart persuaded me to try a motorbike. Petrified, I made it down one hill. When he saw the expression on my face, he took pity on me and agreed I should go back to the hotel.

"You go on ahead," I insisted. "I'll be happy at the swimming pool."

After a short swim, the pains began. I went back to our room and crawled in bed.

"Call the front desk," the maid suggested. "They'll give you a doctor's name."

By the time Mart returned I had managed an appointment. After examining me, the doctor - clad in blue Bermuda shorts - extended his hand to Mart. "Congratulations."

"What do you mean?" he managed to ask, thinking I was pregnant.

"I hear you're celebrating your anniversary. Not many make it to thirty anymore."

"Oh. Yes," Mart stammered in relief. It was momentary, for I was very ill.

"Make sure she stays in bed," the doctor ordered.

So it was that I celebrated our big day - sipping medicine rather than Champagne.

"This bouquet the kids sent is timely. It will look great at my funeral." Me, trying to sound loose. But when the time for our departure rolled around, I insisted I felt well enough to travel. I'd changed my mind about dying there and being buried picturesquely.

Times like this, even an atheist would believe in God, for the heavens intervened and produced such a show of violence the plane was not allowed to land in the Bahamas. Instead of a long delay there, with my abscess threatening to burst, it went directly to Miami, where our car was parked. At least now I was home. Before week's end - I was in surgery.

Grace was a faithful friend while I recuperated. "I made some chicken soup for your lunch." (Enough for a week's worth). About the time I was feeling lonesome and penned in, she appeared at the door again with a bouquet of gardenias.

"Come in. Come in," I greeted. "After surviving the operation I was about to die from cabin-fever. You just saved my life."

Time put me back in action. When I was through chairing the assembly I was asked to plan a program on the water problem for the League of Women Voters. A speaker must be found. Logistics and publicity arranged. Another year rolling to an end.

Gotta have a coffee break with Grace - waving to the lonely figure sitting on her front porch. *Soon as our guests are gone.*

By then it was Christmas. Grace and her husband went to Atlanta to spend it with their kids. After that I didn't see them working in the yard together. Not until a rainy spring day when the new sofa bed was delivered for our front den.

"Let's sleep in here tonight," I said to Mart, "and try it out."

I snuggled in below the open windows, set to watch a movie. The rustle of palm fronds and long leaves from the umbrella tree, together with the beating rain, competed for the sound.

Night noises in another room are different, I thought as the roar of the train at nearby Dixie Highway seemed to be moving down our street. It sounded closer as the volume rose. Descriptions of tornadoes flashed across my mind.

"Mart! A tornado's coming down our street."

In an instant he was in the room – turning off the TV and winding shut the louvered windows. An explosion of light outside – then everything was dark. My California earthquake instinct took over. I ran to an inside doorway and prayed.

The tornado traveled right above the house – then turned. When we felt it was safe, we went outside to see if anything was damaged.

"Would you look at that," said Grace's husband when we met out at the side.

Our shared key lime tree lay toppled on the grass – completely uprooted.

"Musta come right through here – missing both our houses," he added.

"Haven't seen you lately," I said to Grace after we had compared our sensations.

"I've been in the hospital."

"The hospital! What's the matter?"

"I found some lumps when we got home from Christmas. They removed a couple. Trying treatment for the others."

"Oh, Grace. I'm so sorry. Why didn't you let me know?"

"I didn't want to bother you. You're always so busy."

"Don't be silly. What are neighbors for?"

What indeed? I thought later. *What kind of neighbor am I if it takes a tornado to let me see her need?*

After that I made a point to call or drop in for a visit once in a while. But as her health progressed, more and more time elapsed between my calls. *She was so good to me when I was sick. I must take time to visit her.*

"We're going to Carolina for a week," I said to her husband one day. "Will you watch the place?"

"I had to put her back in the hospital. They're doing more tests."

"Oh, no. I'll try and stop to see her."

She lay there sleeping – looking thankful for a chance to rest. I didn't have the heart to wake her. When we came back from Carolina – she was gone.

ONE SMALL STEP

Edith turned off the tape recorder and the music stopped. "Perfect," she said. "Time to call it quits."

We had been rehearsing our modern dance routines – barefoot, a la Isadora Duncan – in the church hall for a performance next day at the annual Interfaith Luncheon held in the local temple.

"Don't forget," Edith said, going out the door. "They told us to come early and eat lunch. And remember – blue leotards and tights with both skirts – the shorter red one on top."

This is going to be different than dancing for some sleepy old folks – like we did last month, I thought as I sat on the floor putting on my shoes. What makes me think I can perform for a bunch of women?

Next day, as I headed west on Oakland Park, I felt my stomach make a fist. What if I fall – like I almost did last time?

The day was brilliant, typical of South Florida, even for the recent cold snap. The orange groves had been spared a freeze and spring was threatening to appear.

I was given a complimentary ticket and a name tag at the registration table. I entered the main section and paused to get my bearings until I spotted Edith – her silver hair glowing -- and took a seat beside her.

The chairlady went to the microphone. "Welcome to our Interfaith Luncheon.

We are happy to see so many here. Let us join Rabbi Weis as he gives the blessing."

When he was finished a waiter came and whispered in his ear. The rabbi followed him out of the hall.

The click of knives and forks was soon drowned in ladies' conversations, augmented here and there with lilt of laughter. Scent of rolls and melted butter mingled with hot coffee in an aura of warm peace. The rabbi returned, and rapped a glass for quiet. Peace became replaced by mild curiosity. Some lingered with their conversation. Others sipped their tea.

"I have some tragic news," he said as the attention heightened. "Soon after blast off this morning The Challenger exploded into bits. The astronauts are all dead."

"Ohhhhhh!" came a cry of unity – a unity of grief.

The hush was soon replaced by formless words expressed in tears. Frantic feelings seen in foolish phrases.

"We must pray for their families. I will keep you informed," the rabbi said.

Shortly after that the waiters brought dessert and the rabbi rose to give his talk. "We are all torn apart with this news, but perhaps our program will bring some sense of peace to this tragedy and so we will continue as planned." He had prepared his message on the safe ground of Psalms and Proverbs. Neither the Christians nor the Jews could take offense. Yet the peace had been shattered like the shuttle.

Disturbed and restless now, I wished we didn't have to perform. It seemed out of keeping with the tragic mood. I waited breathlessly at the edge of the section cleared for our performance – only half hearing the chairlady's announcement of our program.

"We have with us today the Inter-Faith sacred dancers – "Daughters of Friendship."

I felt myself grow weak and giddy. My heart began to wobble. Edith pressed the button for the tape. No more time to fret. We took our places and began.

I felt my heart explode as I whirled in time to "Praise Him." It softened with the slow, almost sensual movements of "The Lord's Prayer" and rose to heights of peace as we danced to the "23rd Psalm." It was during "Antiphon," that I heard my bare foot skid across the floor – an echo from my heart. Edith's moving solo of "Queen Esther" followed. It was over. We curtseyed and returned to our table. I rehashed the steps and felt again that awful moment when I skidded. At last I tuned in to the chairlady who was announcing the next event – a musical comedienne.

Another time and place and mood – the woman might have been a hit. Now, the weakness of her wit was matched by the weak response – brave attempts at laughter and applause.

Remembering how I felt when I almost fell, I empathized, yet I felt embarrassed by the crassness of the jokes. The lunch, which I had eaten tossed inside my stomach. I squeezed my napkin in a ball and watched the women in charge put their heads together in agitated whispers.

What can they do? I reasoned. *It's too late to stop her. Maybe she hasn't even heard about the shuttle.*

The comedienne marched up and down the stage in mock piety singing, "Onward Christian soldiers – marching as to war." "<u>Christian</u> soldiers?" she asked. "I thought their thing was love – not war."

The Christians in the crowd rebelled. War was declared. One by two and three by four, they picked up their purses and left. Here and there a stalwart group remained to clap half-heartedly.

When the act was over the chairlady thanked the woman for her performance and invited the remaining guests to join in singing the closing hymn printed on the back of the program. The comedienne picked up her program and sang along with the others, "Let there be peace on earth. And let it begin with me."

Yes, I thought when we were finished. Let it begin with me.

I said good-bye to my companions as they headed out the door. Then walking against the dispersing crowd, I sought out the distressed chairlady.

"Thank you," I said, extending my hand. "Thank you for your graciousness and your hospitality."

HOW'S MY BACKHAND?

"Great game," said my friend as we gathered up the extra tennis balls and put our rackets in their cases. "I'm ashamed to admit, I never thought you'd be able to return that tricky serve I made in the last set. You must have been practicing your backhand."

Yes, I thought. *It pays to heed instructions.*

It made me think of a time I had heeded a quotation from the Bible: "Therefore, if thine enemy hunger, feed him; if he thirst, give him drink: for in so doing thou shalt heap coals of fire on his head."

Hot coals brought pictures to my mind from my childhood dreams where I envisioned going to India and seeing snake charmers and barefoot men in dhotis walking on hot coals. A sun-baked sidewalk or pavement is enough to send me screeching and scrambling to the nearest grass. Heaping coals of fire on someone's head sounded so cruel – not at all like a Christian thing to do. Upon reflection I realized that the quote was not about getting revenge. Rather, what it really meant was that deeds of kindness to someone who has wronged us, will cause them to burn with shame – hot enough to compare to coals of fire. My backhand tennis stroke had fired up a similar effect on my friend.

So when I began having trouble with a wrong number/phone call situation, I began practicing my backhand. I say, began, for I was pretty rusty and it took several sessions to perfect it.

It started early one Saturday morning when I was jolted from my planned late sleep by the brash sound of the telephone.

"I'm afraid you have the wrong number," I replied sleepily.

After several calls for haircuts, sets, and manicures, I kept one customer on the line long enough to find out that I was being mistaken for the Cut and Curl Beauty Salon. It seemed the new owner had artistically hand styled his business cards and the six at the end of the number was being mistaken for my eight. More trouble surely lurked ahead.

I grew more and more irritated as the calls woke me from a nap or disturbed my morning coffee break. It didn't help my disposition when my "customers" got angry at me as though it was all my fault. They were sure they had dialed correctly – who was I to answer?

About this time those words about hot coals began to send heat waves into my brain. We were planning a three-week vacation. What will happen to my "customers" when I'm not here to set them straight? So I called the shop and explained the situation. But the owner wasn't in and the message was received rather flippantly by his help.

When I returned and found myself being drawn, dripping wet, from the far end of the pool or in from some project in the yard, by Cut and Curl calls, my desperation led me to try the hot coal theory once again. This time when I called the shop, the owner answered.

He sympathized with my problem and suggested that I leave my phone off the hook. But what about our customers? I thought.

I began to doubt the value of hot coals. My friends all reinforced my feelings.

"Just hang up on them," one said.

"Make an appointment and let the owner stew," suggested another.

"Tell 'em the shop is closed."

It all sounded so delightfully vindictive. But it didn't sound like my hot coals quote.

Perhaps I had heaped my kindness on the wrong offenders. The owner or his staff had not been disturbing my peace. My customers were the culprits. So I turned to them.

"You need to dial a six at the end instead of an eight," I informed each one as they called.

Eventually I gained quite a reputation.

"Oh, you're the lady who gets all those wrong numbers. I'm so sorry that I bothered you."

It has been a long time now, since I had someone ask me for a manicure or haircut. My customers seem to have been shamed into learning the right number. It was a back-handed approach, but it got the ball across the net with a score for Love.

MAMA'S MOVE

It was her call. Blind, arthritic, stubborn – it took her a long time to make it. A long time to admit that she'd have to leave her home before they carried her out in a box. Out of her little yellow house at the end of Mulberry Lane. A perfect Grandma place with a fenced in yard for Spunky – her four-legged companion. Pink Grandma roses bloomed on white pickets, red pyracantha berries on the side, a tall pine graced the back where squirrels played hide and seek with Spunky. A haven for stressed out grandchildren who came out to the suburbs from Berkeley or San Francisco to lounge on her scruffy sofa, pig out on chips and ice cream, enjoy a home cooked meal – relax.

It took me as long to discover that you can help people, hug them, alleviate some of their pain, but no matter how much you love them – you cannot live their lives for them. Ultimately each one must make her own move. Too late I found I was just a soldier in Mama's fight for life. My plans – like the jars and bits of leftovers in my refrigerator – had to be moved around from time to time in order to fit hers in.

Like aging itself, learning that lesson was a slow process. It began when the Bay Area Rapid Transit system took my parent's home on Hillside for the Walnut Creek station. Dad must have sensed he'd not live long. He instructed me to "find her a place near the church – close enough to town so she can walk." I was off and running – the dutiful daughter – trying to organize my mother's life.

Shortly before Dad passed away, my husband took a job in South Florida. Prior to our move it had been easy to run out to Mama's – take her grocery shopping or to lunch, tidy up the house, tote her to the doctor, help her choose new clothes. Fun stuff! Not necessarily needed.

Then – 3,000 miles away – the slow deterioration began to escalate. Moving from cataracts to operations: from thick lens glasses to macular degeneration to a white tipped cane. From keeping house and crocheting afghans to hiring housekeepers and watching the evening news with her ears. Arthritis weakened her legs and knees.

I felt impotent being so far away – unable to pop in to clean the kitchen stove or untangle hangers in her closet. I often wished I could be the one to help her to her feet from the pew or the café bench instead of those "nice strangers." My heart ached as I recalled watching her take off her stockings one night – tying them to the bedpost so she could find them in the morning. Or I'd join her in a laugh as she told how she'd gone to Betty's luncheon complaining that her feet hurt. "No wonder," Betty said. "You've got your shoes on the wrong feet."

Airline tickets once used for her to come visit us were switched around. I'd enter the plane on my return, laden with new information I'd gleaned for my bulging Perrier box on the floor of our guest closet – spilling papers and manila folders. Like some giant rat building a winter's nest, I had been gathering leaves and twigs of data. A number for Karen ($7 an hour – call after 5). One from my son for Shared Housing (Ask for Jack). SHOPPING BY PHONE. Clippings from Aunt Elsie on reverse mortgages. Sandra, next door. Adult "Day Care."Independent Living Resources. Meals on Wheels. Friendly Visitors. Alarm systems.

Time for action. Why bother my brother? He's got his hands full with his family. I can handle it. Since Mama loved company I concentrated on retirement places.

"Times have changed," I said to her. "There are places now where you can have your own apartment with housekeeping services, meals, entertainment, friends. Even happy hours. I think you should move into one of those. Live in style."

Mama didn't think so. "What would I do with Spunky? I'll never give him up."

Lurking close behind that statement was her fear of being trapped in a high rise during a fire or an earthquake. No – she wouldn't move.

"I don't know what I'm going to do," I said to my best friend on one of my trips. "I feel so guilty. The kids and neighbors do more for Mama than I do. She needs more than friendly visits now. She seems so disoriented."

"Have you thought of getting a live in – like we had for my mom?"

"Yes, but live-ins are expensive." I was forever juggling figures trying to make Mama's income last her to the end. What to do? I'd better start searching for a helper first thing in the morning.

As I cleaned up from supper, I flicked the "ON" switch of the garbage disposal and heard a growl from deep inside. Then PLOP! The whole thing dropped out at my feet.

"Great!" I grumbled. "Just what I needed. A chance to waste my time looking for a plumber."

I flicked the switch to "OFF." Shoved the parts inside and closed the door. It was Sunday night – already dark. No point in doing anything till morning. I went to bed and repeated my well worn prayer, "Please, God. Help us find someone to help take care of Mama." Before we were awake the next day, the telephone began to ring. Mama's neighbor.

"Do you know a plumber we can call?" I asked. "The disposal went on the blink last night."

"My friend knows a retired man who did some painting for her. She says he's good at fixing things."

He not only came prepared to fix, but he came with a list of prices, ready to go out and buy a suitable replacement. While he set about installing a new model, I explained my predicament.

"By any chance do you know somebody who could come in and help my mother?"

He not only knew someone – she was also available on the terms and hours we needed. She was not only available – she was trained and experienced with working and caring for the blind. She was not only trained – she was sweet and loving and kind. Fred not only fixed Mama's disposal, he came back from time to time to paint and do the yard.

Best of all, whenever he came to do a job, he made a pot of coffee first and stopped to chat a while. I had gained some time and peace of mind.

For a moment. Always new problems popped up. Another worry. Sitting back in Florida, trying to concentrate on a book, I'd see Mama climbing into the bathtub alone. What if she slips and falls?

Fred to the rescue again via an extended showerhead and a stool that straddled the tub. Using the bars he put up, she could lower herself onto the bench, pull her legs into the tub and – with the showerhead – have a nice warm bath. All by herself. This is where she started singing "Pretty bubbles in the air." And this is where she became the last thing on my mind each night as I went to sleep – feeling her vulnerability across the miles – asking God to watch over her.

"How I wish she'd give up the dog and move!"

"It's her life," my husband would reply. "Let her live it like she wants."

I wrestled with the idea of moving her to a place near us. But what about those hours I wasn't there? Mama had lots of friends. Her house was often filled with visitors. The phone busy with invitations to go out to lunch, church, senior events. Would it be fair to take her away from that vital part of her life? I hesitated too, because her health insurance was not covered in Florida. She had a good deal on it from my dad's retirement.

My brother lived in Southern California where her insurance was valid. He'd been begging Mama to come live with them. She tried it once for a few weeks, but Spunky didn't like it.

After several more housekeepers I realized I couldn't handle this alone. The time had come to ask my brother for some help. He and his wife came up. We scouted out a nice board and care place nearby. As usual – Mama and Spunky won out. We hired another woman to help. Signed up for Meals on Wheels, and went home again, physically and emotionally exhausted.

Then came the late night call from Mama's neighbor telling me she'd had it. In my stupor I didn't know if she meant herself or Mama – until she offered to call 911. A few days before, Mama had heard Spunky going into convulsions and decided it was time to put him to sleep. Her decision caused her to fall apart. I got up and readied for another flight – determined to bring Mama back with me – insurance or no insurance. Before I could make the arrangements she called to say, "I've decided to take your brother up on his offer. They're coming to get me this week."

She'd already cancelled her Meals on Wheels, so I called the hired woman and asked her to come in once a day and fix her meals until my brother got there. But as I was finally beginning to learn – I was not the one in charge. My cousin and his wife happened to be passing through in their RV. They packed Mama up, put her to bed in the back, and drove her to my brother's.

The move meant shorter trips for me to California in which to give my brother and his wife time to get away. Time spent sitting on the arm of Mama's easy chair – reminiscing, playing her favorite music tapes, reading aloud. Sad – happy times. Three years of more degeneration – physical and mental. Stress and strain on my brother and his wife. Until one day she looked at them and said, "Take me to a rest home."

"There's one close to me," I said. "Would you like to come to Florida?"

"Yes. That's what I'd like to do."

A pleasant flight across the states, a night spent in our home, second thoughts taking her next morning to the assisted care home, greetings, introductions, smiles, a happy, "See you tomorrow."

All shattered when I found her next day – completely disoriented, angry, frightened. She grabbed my hand and clutched it in wild desperation. "Where am I? I thought you were lost."

"You're here in Florida – near me. Don't you remember? I brought you to the retirement home yesterday. You seemed happy when I left."

"Take me home with you!" she begged, clutching harder. I caught my breath as though my heart had stopped. What have I done?

"Don't worry," the director said. "She'll calm down."

"It was your idea to come here, Mama – remember? I'm just a mile away. I'll be back to see you. We'll go out to lunch or church. I'll bring you to my house for outings."

Mama's moods rose and fell as she attempted to adjust to her new environment. I'd pop a can of cold Pepsi and a few bananas – her favorite treats – into a bag and feel my heart make a fist as I readied to visit her. What will she be like today?

Some days were pleasant. I'd bring my clipboard and pen and take notes while she told about her childhood. As we laughed and talked, the other residents' eyes filled with envy. Tiny smiles crept into the corners of their lips.

"Who are you?" Mama asked on one of my visits. When I told her I was her daughter she bombarded me with questions in open disbelief. "What's your husband's name? Your father's? Your grandmother's maiden name?"

"Come on, Mama," I said. "I'm taking you to church."

"What church?" she asked triumphantly, as though she'd caught me out.

When I gave the right answer she relented and came along peaceably. Another day I touched her hand when I came in.

"Cherisey – is that you?" she asked. "I'm glad you came. I want to tell you something."

"What, Mama?"

"When I'm gone, I don't want you to be sorry."

"Yes, Mama. I understand what you are saying. I'll be happy for you – that you're in heaven. But I'll be sorry, too."

She gave me a little smile. "You don't understand. Not yet."

Months after she was gone, I knew what she had meant. Don't feel guilty. Those times she had clutched my hand and begged me to take her home would have haunted me forever without her words – "Don't be sorry."

After that she went through a period of sorrow that life had nothing left for her. She began to ask me if I thought it was wrong to pray that God would take her. She talked about my Dad and her own mother – wishing she could be with them.

Not long after, she became bedridden. A growing peace developed. She no longer begged me to stay or take her home. It became a joy to visit her.

"You sound happy," she said one morning.

"I am. We're going on a little trip."

"How nice."

I took her hand in mine, prayed with her, kissed her.

"I have to go now, Mama. I'll be back soon. You've been a good mother to us. Good-bye."

We returned home late from our out of town weekend. The message machine was beeping irritably. I listened half-heartedly as I took notes. "Please call the Retirement Home" jolted me awake. I recognized the nurse's voice and knew.

The attendant told me they had overheard her prayer the day before. Naming each member of our family. Commending each into God's care. In the morning, after being bathed and settled in her bed, she closed her eyes and went to sleep.

Mama's move.

GOODBYE AGAIN

"Don't forget to leave my name with the gate attendant for tomorrow," I said to my young friend, Dorree, before I rang off.

She had suffered from a respiratory illness most of her life and was going through one of her bad spells. I thought it was time to go over to her condo, spruce up the place, and do some shopping for her.

My husband and I had moved from California to Florida in the early seventies – leaving our three grown children behind. It was a wrenching good-bye to closeness in their everyday lives.

I got busy with church connected jobs and League of Women Voters – trying to keep from feeling sorry for myself. My position as an officer in our churchwomen's organization often took me into the church office for supplies or to make copies. Unfortunately, whenever a machine sees me coming, it gets its hackles up and quits working, so I depended on the secretary for help. One day I went in and found a strange person sitting at the desk.

"Where's the secretary?" I asked.

"I'm it," Dorree replied. "They let the other one go."

Dorree was around the age as our children. Her mother was dead and her father lived far away in Wisconsin. I became a steady helper Friday afternoons folding Sunday bulletins and getting acquainted. It didn't take long for a mother/daughter relationship to develop between us. She became a regular participant at our table for dinners and holiday celebrations. She often took me to special events like productions of "Cats" and "Chorus Line – places I couldn't drive to myself. I no longer felt so lonely with a live body to hug in lieu of two daughters 3,000 miles away. Dorree was a small woman and because of her illness – very thin. One hugged her gingerly – afraid of breaking those tiny brittle bones.

Now as I approached the gate I was concerned about her declining health. I entered the complex, parked in my usual spot, and climbed the stairs to her second floor apartment. There was no answer to my knock. I knocked and knocked and called and called. Nothing. I had met her next-door neighbor and so felt free to knock on her door. We tried phoning Dorree's number, but no response. Feeling desperate, I went in search of some help.

"She's got to be in there," I said to the condo administrator. "Her car is still here."

The security officer came with me and unlocked the door. As I headed through the apartment I was grateful for his presence close behind. Green trees from the park across the canal, reflected on the mirrored living room wall, bringing life into the room. When I entered Dorree's bedroom, I was sure that I'd found death. The oxygen tube that she often needed had slipped from her nostrils and her eyes were closed. As I drew nearer I saw that she was still breathing. I called her name and she fluttered her eyelids. We immediately called 911 and watched as the attendants strapped that weak little body onto the gurney. I felt like saying, "Be careful. Don't break her." I followed the ambulance to the hospital and spent the rest of the day there waiting to see if she would make it. After stabilizing her condition they moved her to the critical care unit where she was kept alive on a respirator for several weeks. She improved somewhat, but when they could do no more for her they suggested she spend the rest of her days in a special care center for respiratory patients. She chose what she felt would be a better life – go home, go back to work, live it out.

In the meantime my mother who was in her nineties, legally blind, and unable to walk or take care of herself, decided to move from California to an assisted care facility near me. It was back and forth between them now. Which one needs me most? That was early summer 1994. It was mid October when my mother passed away. At least I still had Dorree. By Thanksgiving Dorree was so weak, she could barely make it through the meal and back home to bed.

Although she never quite said, I got the impression the doctor had told her that without the respirator she could expect to live no longer than a year. If so, time proved him right as she had to quit her job and was in and out of the hospital several times that winter. She talked about going home where her family could take care of her, but Wisconsin is a cold place in February. Could her sick little body take it?

"I'll wait till it gets warmer. Don't tell my sister how bad I am," she pleaded.

At last I took it on myself to inform her sister of her condition. The night before her family arrived I slept on Dorree's living room sofa – afraid I'd hear a death rattle any moment. They managed to move her home to Wisconsin. She never made it through to spring.

WHAT IF?

"I'm sorry to hear about your mastectomy," I said to my mother's German friend.

"Ach, ja. And at mine age!"

In her eighties at the time, I had to agree – not an appealing resolution at the coda of one's life. Now – seventy myself – I wonder, "What if it happens to me?" A question at the tip of every woman's mind.

I've been told I have beautiful breasts. (Aren't they all?) They weren't always so. As a young woman they were scrawny buds. Age has blossomed them out. A bonus I never expected from the passing years. How *would* I react to losing one or both? And how would my husband react? Now, as I wait for the doctor's report of a biopsy taken from my right breast, my first thought is to run out and buy a roll of film. Have my husband take some pictures for his future fantasy and recall.

But he seems more concerned about keeping me than my breast and I end up consoling him. "Don't worry. It's probably benign."

Benign? What if it isn't? Is he right in worrying? Is it a fast growing kind – too far gone already? Should I write my farewell letter to my kids? Then reason returns. Even if it is malignant that doesn't necessarily mean radical mastectomy. But – "What if?" We women often say, "Love *me* – not my body." Yet we do drastic things to keep our bodies beautiful – starve, binge, purge, become anorexic, risk losing our hair by dousing it with dyes and chemicals, clip, oil, shave, expose ourselves to cancer yielding gamma rays, spend more precious time making up our faces than a clown at a circus.

Edging closer to the end one begins to realize that physical change and deterioration are inevitable. Being able to see, hear, walk, and laugh become major events. In my seventy years I've had several major surgeries: appendectomy, leg veins stripped, hysterectomy, gall bladder removal. I recall saying to my doctor, "There's nothing left you dare take out." "Not so," he said. "You've got two kidneys and two lungs. One of each could be removed." He didn't mention breasts. As I wait to hear from the pathologist, my philosophical reasoning departs – leaving me devastated at the thought of it actually happening to me. How or would I cope?

I am brought short by the news from an acquaintance – much younger than I am, wife, mother of two young children. At her regular check-up, without time for a reflective, "What if?" she was slapped into the hospital for a radical double mastectomy. How and will *she* cope?

And then she shows me. Actually writing a lovely note in the middle of her problems, thanking me for my concern and prayers. By being open about her condition. Keeping her sense of humor. By her determination to look the best she can – choosing reconstruction with C cup dimensions this time around. Anticipating short hair – a thing her husband had always vetoed. Trusting God to help her cope as always with the problems life offers.

It might not be as simple as her seven year old implies, "It's okay, Mom. We don't need those things any more, anyway. We're big kids now." Not simple, but she's managing. Managing because she's beyond her own loss to, "What would happen to my husband and children if I lose my life?" What if?

As I discovered long ago – breasts are a bonus in life – not life itself. Anais Nin put it this way, "I postpone death by living, by suffering, by error, by risking, by giving, by losing."

ME AND MY BIOPSY

"Right breast surgical biopsy – scheduled for Tuesday afternoon," the doctor said. Looked like troubled days ahead. The trouble started early when someone at the hospital called the day before to say I'd need to be there by 11:00 am instead of 1:00 pm as I'd been told. Pre-op does take time. And as I found out – energy. Physical as well as emotional.

The time change meant juggling my husband's need for the car with mine. How many times hadn't he said, "Don't make the appointment for Tuesday morning. I have to have the car." By this time, I was ready to walk rather than change the date. Lucky for me his meeting got out early and I was driven to my fate. Seeing the crowded parking lot I decided it might have been better if I *had* walked. We finally ended up using valet parking. Good heavens! I'm here for a biopsy – not a fancy dinner.

"Oh well," I said with my best "I can cope with this," attitude. "We're here and that's what counts."

I zipped past the desk on the left where I had been instructed to go – straight to the one in the center – zapped back again. The attendant wore a pleasant smile and nice clothes, but she couldn't find my name on the list. After several spellings, searches from A - Z's, and a brief moment of panic, (thinking I'd have to start all over again with appointments), she found it – right where it always is – at the end of the page.

Next a smiling lady led me to a door about an inch away. (It would have been a lot to ask the list lady to handle that, too). The woman let me through, but barred the way from my husband. "You can't go in there!"

"Why not?"

"There aren't enough chairs."

I took my place in the one vacant chair, felt him hover above my right shoulder, and knew he'd made one of his famous power plays again.

The woman admitting me was new at her job, so Mrs. Director of Doorways stood by to help. There we were, all four of us, clustered about that tiny desk – flustering the poor new lady. I'm not the only one in trouble today, I thought. She has her problems – I've got mine. We were practically sisters. Until – looking at the bracelet she'd attached to my right wrist, I discovered my name was spelled wrong.

That did it! Everyone – at least in the whole south wing – got involved in correcting the misspelling. Admitting gave up and sent me to a small office in pre-op where I was met with a gruff, "Who are you?"

Yes. Who am I? Did we come to the wrong room? Then braving it, I told her my name was Wyneken, but they've got me down as Wyneker. "I'll go along with that," I added. "I've answered to worse."

"No! No! It has to be corrected."

Corrected – on a clipboard thick with papers bearing my name. It looked to be a job too big for the office woman, so she shunted me on to pre-op where I was fitted with a new name tag on my left wrist (where it should have been in the first place). Once again my husband was barred from entry. Like I said before, I'd come there that morning wearing my best "I can cope with this" attitude. It was beginning to weaken. I say beginning. We're a long ways yet from OR.

There were three beds in the ambulatory room and as many nurses. Plus the supervisor. It could have been so simple.

"You take A. You take B. You take C. And I will supervise."

But no. They decided to play musical chairs. When the music stops, go to the next patient. One woman provided the music by singing. Another made a fuss about placing the identifying bracelets and IV's opposite the operating side. So when she began readying my right hand for the IV, I cleared my throat, got up my nerve, and said, "I thought it was supposed to go on the left side." That was bad enough, but after remedying that situation, she began looking for the tubing and connector. Finding the packet opened, lying on a shelf, she quipped, "Is this sterile?" (Was it A or B or C who had been so efficient?) I definitely began to lose confidence. Watching two nurses try to get the needle in my room partner's vein, I lost even more. After two vain requests for someone to let my husband in, I put my book into the plastic bag along with my clothes. All too stressful to concentrate on "Essays on Poetry."

In "holding" they put me beside my roommate and I watched two more nurses poke around at her before they finally succeeded in getting the needle in her vein. Meanwhile the nurse in charge of holding – sang, talked to herself, and made a business deal with a co-worker over installing 400 new toilets in the place where she lives.

In OR at last – so clean and green and efficient – I scooted onto the operating table figuring now I could relax. But it was just like home – the phone began to ring and the OR nurse went off to chat. Is no place sacred anymore? By then I half expected a call from one of the local funeral parlors, offering me a special on grave sites. And of course the nurse wasn't ready for the doctor when he arrived. His, "Next time you won't answer the phone," satisfied my sense of righteousness as I drifted out.

I drifted back in to the tune of uncertainty as the nurses discussed which room the orderly should put me in. He listened to the discourse a few minutes, then made a major decision to put me back in my corner by the window. In the meantime my husband had been asking, "Where is Mrs. Wyneken?"

"Oh, she's the one with the double mastectomy?"

"NO!"

"Oh, she's the one with the knee replacement?"

"NO!"

He finally found me there in the hall – being wheeled into my room. This time they let him in – along with the doctor and his diagnosis: "CANCER" – said with efficiency and authority in a sympathetic tone.

I BRING MY BOOK – PREPARED TO WAIT

      I bring my book – prepared to wait. And wait I do – in stages. First to register – then down the hall to the waiting room. A quick detour through a cubbyhole where I take off my blouse and bra, don a dark blue gown, and settle in – to wait.
      At last I hear my name being called (mangled as usual) along with directions to Room 1. The attendant directs me to lie on a stretcher-like table. Measurements are made. My breast is marked with blue pencil. A tattoo is etched between them. A mark for future reference. Radiation begins.

FLEEING FLOYD

Determined as a school of salmon swimming up stream to spawn, Floyd made his way across the Atlantic – aimed at Ft. Lauderdale. The storm never reached us – yet it left a strong impact on my mind.

We'd been watching its approach for days on the weather channel – faithfully recording its coordinates on our hurricane map (supplied yearly by our neighborhood Publix supermarket). The closer it got the more jittery we felt. Since Hurricane Andrew, evacuation areas had been extended from the coast, leaving us well within the designated area. No problem with Andrew. Our young friend lived out of the zone. "Come stay with me," she'd said. Since then, she had passed away. What will we do this time? Where will be go? Shelters were being offered in nearby schools – but were we up to camping out on a gymnasium floor with a room full of strangers? We went to bed with those questions filling our minds.

Morning arrived with Floyd trailing close behind. We made up our minds at last. A quick scan of the Florida AAA book and a call to Naples on the west coast, produced the last available reservation – a suite – at the Best Western. Even though it was more expensive, I secretly rejoiced at the suite part – knowing my husband's detestation of small quarters. I left orders for a late arrival. We still had lots to do.

First on the list – hurricane shutters. Beastly things. Heavy. Numbered for individual windows. Needing a heavy hand or an electric screwdriver. It was summer and hot. My husband is not young. Not as young as the man across the street who took pity on two seniors and offered to help – freeing me to carry patio chairs to the garage, cover the pool filter, bring in the garbage dumpster, do back ups on my computer. Shall I roll up our oriental rug and get it off the floor? Cover my computer?

Put my back-up discs in the freezer? Do we have enough water? Do I have time to shop for more tuna and canned fruit? Why didn't I go earlier? Shall I bring some food along? And speaking of tuna – I'd better make the guys some lunch.

A steady clank, clank followed them around the house as they maneuvered the heavy aluminum shutters. Darkness followed inside. I felt trapped.

Several hours later – shutters attached, bags and cooler packed, water, water heater, coffee pot, computer turned off – we waved to Ed – working on his shutters – and headed west on Alligator Alley. A steady stream of traffic accompanied us – at a steady pace – all fleeing Floyd.

"No empty rooms in town," the motel clerk said as we signed in. We felt thankful for our spot. As I settled in, my husband went to check out the adjoining restaurant. Suit and ties required. At a motel restaurant? We weren't prepared for that. But they said to come on over – they'd put us in a corner out of sight. And they did. By the next morning Floyd had veered north away from Ft. Lauderdale, but we decided to make sure, and stayed another night. It gave us a chance to explore the Naples area – something we had never done.

Home again – day three – we set about reversing our preparations. Removing shutters from the vital windows – leaving some up. The season wasn't over yet. Crabby and let down from being on a high so long, the dust and grime from the shutter project, irritated me enough to hose down the patio and give the furniture a good cleaning before putting it back in place. Plenty of clean water.

Next morning when I took my bath, the water seemed quite tepid. By dishwashing time I realized the heater wasn't working. Had turning it off done it some harm? Had the hurricane left us with a problem after all?

A new water heater was recommended by the plumber. That was Friday. No delivery until Monday. A whole weekend of teakettle baths and dish washing. Treks through the house toting scalding water. When it comes to cleaning – bodies or clothes – there's nothing like good hot water to open the pores. I began to complain. "Such inconvenience."

"Be glad we have water," said my husband.

And yes, I recalled that after Hurricane Andrew tap water was contaminated in many areas for several days. Yes, I should be thankful.

I thought about my reaction again recently when we saw the movie, "Shower." It depicts a family in a drought torn area of China, going from farm to farm, trading bowls of much needed grain for bowls of water. Not for their sustenance, but to fill a bath for their daughter's wedding preparations as prescribed by their tradition. And I had complained about lukewarm water?

Somewhere I read that giving thanks in the midst of sickness or trouble – is the best medicine. Like the hot water with bodies and clothes – giving thanks opens the pores of our perspective and gets rid of the dirt. I had much to be thankful for in connection with Floyd. A house untouched – clean water – a kind neighbor. And two nights off from cooking.

SPLAT!

"Would you put a floodlight in a sick room?" the pastor asked – trying to bring home the point that we each have specific talents to offer – in specific places. I've remembered his words over the years, yet I confess I've often been guilty of wishing I were someone else. Someone smart – beautiful – talented – young. A floodlight.

Until that balmy March evening while visiting friends in Chicago. We had just finished dinner in the open air section of John Barleycorn – a favorite neighborhood restaurant – and were heading home via Cleveland Avenue and the bookstore to browse.

"What a gloomy looking place," someone said as we passed Grant Hospital.

"At least they're open," I remarked.

Our friend, Judith, is younger than me and has long legs (The kind my uncle would have died for). She has a lot of energy and knows how to get right to the meat of a situation. We were walking – so the thing to do was walk. Straight to our goal. No ambling. Leaning forward – scuttling along beside her – I attempted to keep up.

"You'd better slow down," my husband called from behind.

I was having none of that "old woman" business. I could keep up with the youngest and the best. Then SPLAT – I fell flat on my face. I lay there for a while in a sort of daze – feeling blood trickle from my lips and cheek. Wondering if I'd broken my glasses – if my eyes had been injured. A young couple came by – concerned and helpful in getting me to my feet. Blood dripped from my gouged thumb – splattering red marks on my green dress. My husband bent my glasses back in shape. Then he and my friend led me home – one on each arm.

Judith marched me into the bathroom to wash off and cover my wounds with anti-biotic salve – Bactoderm for dogs – left over from Gilbert's recent operation. Then she settled me on the living room couch. Gladys – the other Shih Tzu lap dog – joined me there to help me bear my aching thumb.

"Do you think we ought to get it X-rayed," says Judith.

Not me. But good sense prevailed. She called in her neighbor – an OB specialist to convince me. The "ayes" had it and we trekked back to Grant Hospital where we spent our evening in ER – no longer making snide remarks – just happy it was there and open. First a police report must be made because I fell on a city sidewalk. Then after several X-rays my hand was put into a cast up to my elbow. My nose was pronounced fractured.

In a state of shock – all I wanted to do was put a paper bag over my head and curl into a corner. But we were visiting friends. Plans had been made. So out I went next morning to the Norman Rockwell show at the Chicago Historical Society – wearing my bloodied face and whatever outfit my cast permitted, (I hadn't packed with that in mind). The grown-ups did a good job of not staring, but it was too much to ask of kids. And about the time our lunch waiter managed to ignore my wounds, my husband had to go and ask, "Does it look like I beat up on her?" (Beep – Beep. Look at her!) A stroll through Washington's Mount Vernon exhibit ended with an openly shocked doorman – followed by, "God bless you."

Sores on and in my mouth, plus no good cutting leverage, found me ordering pumpkin soup for dinner at the lovely gourmet Pond Restaurant in nearby Lincoln Park where I had looked forward to dining. Sunday took us south to a church called Holy Family, where the preacher is a friend of our friend. True to its name, the people were warm and accepting. I felt enfolded by healing arms as Butch twice laid his hands on me and blessed me.

An entertaining production of "Forever Plaid," pork chops smothered in gorgonzola cheese, a tour of the Titanic exhibit, and a trek through 505, the captured German submarine at the Museum of Science and Industry, didn't help me forget my hideousness. If ever there was a time for me to wish I were someone else, this was it.

After Butch's blessings and my return home, my facial wounds healed remarkably fast and well, but their impact left a mark I hope will never be erased. It reminds me to be satisfied with who I am – not try to keep up with someone younger who has long legs, someone who is smart, beautiful, talented, or I might fall – SPLAT on my face.

TIDE POOLS

"Don't forget to see the tide pools," our son called as we waved good-bye.

My thoughts went back to our honeymoon and many other happy times searching for treasures among the tide pools along the California coast. They had always been a special part of our trips to that area – promising to show us secrets from deep within the sea. The tide never failed.

We were on our way to Acadia National Park in Maine. According to our son the tide pools are fantastic there and I aimed to see them. I could almost hear the roar of rollers chase each other – the hiss as they broke on rock – feel the spray on my cheek. See green-tressed seaweed maids curtsey to the cresting waves.

"You aren't going to pull one of your "it's too late" control tactics when we get to the park and tide pools – are you?" I asked Mart.

"You make me sound like a villain."

"Sometimes."

Mart and I had been married forever. I'd become a pro at balancing. When to talk – when to turn it off – when to push for something – when to let it lie. We drove along in our brown Mercedes – silent. Mart, at the wheel since four AM, stared at the road ahead, probably hearing Bach's Fugue in D, not breakers.

Buttercups spilled yellow across green fields. Pink and purple larkspur filled roadside gutters with their steepled spires. Ads displayed phrases I'd never seen before: barn sales, Kayaks For Sale, whale watching tours by air. We crossed onto L'Isle des Monts Desert. Mart reached into the side pocket for the AAA Travel Book and handed it to me. "I've marked a few motels I think are good. Watch for one of them."

I gave him a salute.

105

He darted me a quick look. "You want to choose? Go ahead. See how easy it is without studying first."

Give him a break, I thought. He's tired. "Here's a nice one in Bar Harbor," I replied.

"Too far from the ferry. We want to catch the first one out to Nova Scotia in the morning. Here's one that I checked – Hillside Inn with view." He pulled in.

"Looks good. Guess your planning does pay off."

Mart registered. Brought in the luggage. "Let's drive into Bar Harbor and check out a place to eat tonight. Going to treat you to some real Maine lobster."

"I thought we were going to the park."

"I need some gas."

I looked at my watch. "Will there be time to stop at the tide pools?"

"Yeah. Sure."

We freshened up. Drove into Bar Harbor. Hunted out a place to eat lobster. Watched the boats perch on the bay like a flock of ibis in the Everglades. Circled past the old inn presiding over the scene like a dowager. Pulled into a gas station. Mart and the old timer filling the tank began to talk.

You'd think they were long lost friends. He's stalling – tide pools were never in his plans.

"Let's check out the information center first," he said as we entered Acadia Park.

"Now? How come you're suddenly interested in Information Centers?"

Hands full of pamphlets and maps, we began circling the one-way road. Slim white-skinned birch trees peeped wide-eyed from deep within sun-specked woods. Cottonwoods turned silver dollar leaves – catching the echo of a jingling breeze. Wild roses, rouged cerise, flirted along the path. Frenchman's Bay lay quiet – drenched in blue.

It's not like I imagined – but it has a certain balance. "Here," I said, pointing to a long stretch of accessible beach. This looks like a good place to stop."

Mart kept driving.

"How about here?"

"Uh-uh."

"You're going too fast. We pass the pools before we see them."

"Uh-huh."

I reached for the park map. "A good spot's coming up. Slow down."

"Everyone else thinks so, too. Look at the crowd."

"So what?"

"There isn't room to park."

We drove on in silence until we came to a section of the shore lined with huge smooth boulders.

"STOP. I'm going to look – even if you're not." Mart pulled to the side of the road. "I'll wait."

"Whatever."

I turned onto a roadside path toward an opening in the brush and struck out across the boulders for the shore. At last I was down – standing at the edge. No shallow pools spawning sea anemones and starfish. No crashing waves – just the ones inside. What makes him think he can always have his way?

I watched the water lap beneath my feet. The quiet backwash roll calmed my angry feelings. Andante and allegro – a steady ebb and flow. It reminded me of my dad's oft-repeated advice: "Marriage isn't a 50/50 proposition. It's more like 75/75." Good and bad overlapping – like the waves. Some garbage had drifted into my day, but sea anemones and starfish would be there, too. Once again the ocean had brought me a treasure. A wider view that helped me cope with my problems at hand. The tide never fails.

"Nice – isn't it?" someone behind me says.

I turn. Lose my balance.

"Careful." A virile grey-haired man reaches out to steady me.

His hand feels gentle on my arm. His grasp quick. A spark of warmth creeps through me. Tense, I look down at his hand. "Yes – nice."

He stares at me and releases it. "I like what the tide brings in."

I feel my blood move through me – a tide below.

A young woman peers over the top of a boulder. "Oh there you are, Dad. Come on – we're heading back."

Dad follows his daughter – then turns. Gives me a nod. "The tide never fails."

I see them top the rise and disappear. Sit down at the edge and watch the water lap beneath my feet. *Good and bad – each wave overlapping.* I smile remembering the pulse of Mart's reach in bed that morning. *We've had a good life together. Never could stay mad for long. Why spoil our day?* Equilibrium restored, I feel the need to stabilize the balance between us and head back towards the road. No Mercedes. *Now what?*

I look both ways. *No point in going back. It's a one-way road. Maybe he stopped ahead and is waiting.*

I trudge along the roadside so I won't miss the car and spot another couple coming toward me. "Is your name Cherise? Your husband is heading toward those cliffs – looking for you."

Does he think I could have walked that far already? He must be getting frantic.

Nothing to do but keep plodding on. I come to a fork in the road – one upper and one lower – both going the same direction. Afraid I'd miss him by taking the wrong one, I plop down on a rock to wait till he comes back.

It'll take him forever to come back around. I thought he meant to wait for me. We should have discussed it.

The pressure of curious glances from passers-by draws me forward to the crest of the hill where I spot the parked Mercedes. Just as I step out to cross, I'm forced back by an approaching car. I look up to see Mart, sitting in the back seat of a police car.

The officer laughs. "Lost and found – one wife."

"Hi." I smile at Mart.

He smiles back. The tide never fails.

COLOR – TRAVEL AND NATURE

A FRENCH REVOLUTION

"You can just catch the last tour," said the uniformed man selling tickets at the 15th century castle in Loches, France. The group had already descended the cold, stone stairs and were listening to the guide describe the cell in which they stood.

"Let's go on by ourselves," I suggested to Mart. "We can't understand French anyway."

We continued down the narrow stone passageway – curving and descending to the dungeons: ghastly, ghostly, cell-like caverns – hewn from living rock. We could hear the tour group talking and walking about above us. Then a door slammed. A key turned in a lock. Silence. The next instant all the lights went out.

We're locked in," I screamed. "We're locked in for the night! It was the last tour!"

"Stand still," said Mart as he fumbled for a match. "We'll find the wall and feel our way."

"Help! Help!" we called. "Help! Help!"

An eternal moment of terror imagining rats crawling on our bodies through a long cold night beneath a dripping rock-carved ceiling. Then in a flash the lone bulb came on. We heard the sound of footsteps above us again.

"The guide must have been demonstrating what it was like in the dark for the prisoners," I reasoned.

We ran back up the stairs and joined the tour. The people looked at us and tittered.

They did it on purpose," I whispered to Mart.

"Nooo! Don't be silly."

But creeping inside came a feeling – not unlike the dungeons – we were safe, but we were prisoners. Prisoners of a Cold War.

FLORIDA LIVING

Baby's breath of pink permeates the morning with blush of baby rose. I waken to red cardinal's staccato wake-up call. Like background musak, a bird I've not yet sighted, reiterates the message with its nagging call – taroo, taroo, taroo.

I take some fresh squeezed orange juice to the patio for my morning matins. Hear the wind strum palm fronds, sizzle bushes, whistle through the screens. Black grackles – sparkling iridescent blue – stalk the grass, leveling the scene with a keeper's eye. Black and yellow orioles vie for a piece of hedge. Blue jays dive and grab in bold foray. Doves coo shyly in soft tones. Words rise like wings on wind drafts in silent unseen splay.

Dollops of whipped cream, floating in a bowl of blue, hover above me defying gravity with their heavy fullness. Or perhaps some woman, in her hurry to clean up, spilled a bag of cotton balls and let them drift across the sky.

Red crested cardinals flange the hedge, busy building nests in the orange trees. Not to be out-done, one has twined his with a label from Saks. Another winged guest calls, "Luigi! Luigi!" Poor guy. With a nag like that, I'd hide, too. Mockingbirds entertain with endless repertoires. One in particular catches my ear – trilling songs of swamp birds. Did she flee from fires in the Everglades?

Flocks of parrots – bright green bodies, black-feathered tails and wings, red beaks and feet – appear from time to time. Their raucous screams and assertive manners drive my backyard menagerie away.

Thick, long-fingered St. Augustine grips the grains of sand below – spreading a green carpet for variegated crotons, orange and red hibiscus, gardenias. Yellow allamanda blossoms cling along the fence. Red impatiens bloom from hanging pots – starlets seeking audience and fame.

Lemons – bigger than oranges – brighten the scene from the neighbor's yard. Scent of orange blossom, jasmine, and gardenias follows me as I take my daily laps in the swimming pool. Little lizards creep among the ferns or crawl up on the screens. Frogs no bigger than a nail head – scoot beneath the screen door and hop into the water. Squirrels – our resident clowns – amuse with trapeze artist tricks: balancing the cable wire as they scurry from an angry mother bird, deftly maneuvering the fence top with a large walnut in their mouths, or scampering across the patio screen in a noisy game of chase.

Now a darkened sky. A gentle drop of rain. Thunder grumbles as it stumbles by. Then suddenly – a storm. It charges through the house – banging doors, fluttering the blinds, scattering papers, sweeping clutter from its path. Opening the trap door in the sky it washes the patio with a sheet of water – thick and straight like a woman letting down her long white hair. Leaving in its wake spattered glass and tousled leaves. Bringing back the grackles – to chat on the wires.

What do they find to talk about? Is it "current" events – gleaned from airways through their feet? Or do they speak of things banal? Remarking how the grapefruit hang heavy on the tree. Taking time to note the movement and the yellow. Pointing to the squirrels racing on the fence. Capturing scents of life. Enjoying daylight's fade into pumpkin pink – blended with persimmon.

Dark creeps inland from Atlantic shores. Purple clouds back-stoop day where they meet the bluescaped western sky. The sky is dark above the bougainvillea – yet through the neighbor's tree I see a glow. White blooms burst with Jasmine scent. The hedgerow is alive. Day is passing over – redolent with rise.

FOR THE BIRDS

If I believed in reincarnation I'd have to say I once had wings. Why else would I be so enamored with such a motley group of critters – arrayed in more colors, sizes, and shapes than shoes in a Payless store. They've winged their way with me from the prairies of Dakota, to the San Francisco Bay Area, and on to Florida. Although each move introduced different birds, they were a constant in a changing world – offering me a Symphony in Wing Major with its overture and movements – adagio, presto, allegretto, allegro, and andante.

My passion began with the meadowlark. As a child on the Dakota prairie, I often went barefoot. Dirt settled in between my toes. The meadowlark's song of "Wash-my-feet-we-do" made a lot of sense – beyond the lyric tune. But my sympathy went to sparrows taking refuge in flight – escaping Rex, our dog.

My bird watching began in earnest when I was a mother of four living in North Oakland in the San Francisco Bay Area. An elderly couple lived next door. Friendships grew between the young and old via waves and smiles. Their parrot was the main attraction. On warm days they put Polly in the open window for fresh air and sun. The parrot's pea green feathers shimmered in the light. Her dark eyes, surrounded by a circle of white, resembled the sunflower seeds she loved to eat. "Not it! Not it!" she called – long after the children went inside.

Our move to San Carlos Avenue in the hills of Piedmont introduced me to starlings. Whole communities of them held conventions in the tall cedar tree between our house and the neighbor's. One was assigned to baby sit the youngsters perched on telephone wires while the delegates debated in loud tones. A handclap brought the meeting to a silent standstill – resumed in an instant. Our son and the boy next door took particular pleasure in delaying the proceedings.

Our first pet bird made her entrance in that house. It was a gift from our daughter's third grade school-mate, moving to Japan. Not a good move for Tweety Bird. Her only remains – a yellow feather inside the tipped cage – after an unexpected visit from the neighbor's cat. Who says cats can't open doors?

A short divided street, San Carlos bordered Magnolia at one end, Oakland Avenue the other. Robins fed on berries from pyracantha bushes that graced the manicured center strip between the upper and lower one-way levels. But it was the mourning doves from nearby Oakland Avenue that drew my attention – dropping funeral dirges down the open chimney of my soul.

Another move took us higher in the hills to St. James Drive. The house was built on the down slope of Indian Creek. The creek spilled through the backyard, tumbling at the edge in a twelve foot waterfall. Pink, white, blue, and green hydrangeas, purple fuchsias, and red pyracantha berries bloomed along its side. Tall California laurel and live oak reached three floors up to my kitchen window. They offered me view of a robin's nest, two blue eggs, and a noisy battle between Mama Bird and a marauding squirrel. Counter attacks with a wet dishrag failed to save the eggs.

Red-breasted robins stripped the red berries from the pyracantha bushes, dipped into the creek in drunken orgy, and mistook the new washed windows for the sky. The air was filled with boisterous flapping wings.

Somehow a lone bird got trapped inside our house the day Pop died. It fluttered frantically from our grasp – lurching toward light from the windows. An eerie sensation. Was it Pop? Come to tell us, "Don't hold on to me. I'm heading for eternal light." Pop was a preacher.

A feeling came over me one day as I sat in my lower level sewing room. Someone's watching! I faced the window as I worked on my machine. A dark day. Soft rain. Quiet. My glance went up. Met the stare of a large owl – perched and puffed on a gnarled limb of the live oak. A judge on his courtroom bench. I shivered.

About that time we took a trip to Jamaica. A morning's drive to Anchovy found us spellbound in Miss Lisa Solomon's Bird Sanctuary. A scraggly enclosure – surrounded by potted palms, ferns, pink hibiscus, and colorful crotons. Miss Lisa sat us – one at a time – in her one weather-beaten chair. She placed a small bottle of sugar water in our hand. "Take your other hand and poke your finger toward the tip. Be very still." A brief moment of quiet waiting brought a delicate iridescent, green-breasted, red-beaked, long-tailed, hummingbird who lit on our finger and fed. Yellow birds of Caribbean song pecked on grain strewed on the ground. Magical. Perhaps Miss Lisa had been a bird once, too.

Our move to South Florida brought us to a paradise – filled with birds. Our backyard, once a sanctuary, still offers daily concertos. Snowy egrets feed near waterways that line the roads or blossom in roosts on Florida Holly trees. Cattle graze – oblivious to the cowbirds pecking insects from their backs. Red heads bobbing, common gallinules paddle freely in local swamps and lakes. A visit to tradewinds Park always rewards me with screeching peacocks vying to display their tails.

No out of state visitor escapes my personal tour of Everglades National Park. Endless spreads of green, tinged with oaten sawgrass were once snow-capped with white egrets. But women needed plumes for hats. "Snow birds" from the north need water. Condos, adorned with green lawns year around, inch the dike deeper and deeper into that River of Grass. Depleting the supply of water. Despoiling the ecosystem. Swamp birds huddle near the sloughs. Bent beaked ibis and roseate spoonbills tease gators to the shore.

Graceful blue herons and American bitterns stand statue-still, stalking unsuspecting bass. Lacking oil in their wings, brown, white winged anhinga perch in red gumbo limbo trees and spread their wings to dry for another dive. Crows, waiting for a picnic morsel at Paurotis Pond, stand around and gossip – wrapping blue black wings in the apron of their arms. Purple gallinules hide among the reeds. Shy of cameras seeking pictures of their purple throated undersides displayed beneath green backs.

One cold Christmas Eve we opened our front door – heading to Loxahatchee National Wildlife Reserve to show our guests the birds. Next to our car stood a large egret. Long legs straight, dressed in his white uniform, waiting like a doorman.

Was he inviting me to enter? Be a bird?

LA BOMBA

November 1971 – last stop on a Pacific Rim tour – the Philippines. We were on our way to visit my husband's brother, Jerry, who was a missionary there. It had been thrilling to visit Japan: ride the new Tokaido line – a fast train from Tokyo to Kyoto, sleep on a mat on the floor in a Japanese ryocan, eat so much fish that we began to smell like it, take a Japanese style bath – soaping first, then dipping into the steaming tub, visit the lovely temples and their manicured gardens, and watch prayers go heavenward as people's penciled requests fluttered gaily on the whitened prayer tree. A pleasure to rent a car and tour the island of Taipei, past fields where peasants winnowed rice and sharp mountain peaks loomed like those we'd seen in Chinese paintings and find a pot of hot steaming tea in our hotel room welcoming us to lovely Sun Moon Lake. It was an adventure in culture shock as we wended our way through throngs of teeming humanity amid bright signs and colorful market stalls lining the streets of Hong Kong. It was a meaningful experience when I became ill and learned how foreigners were treated with concern and care here in this far away place.

For just as we were scheduled to fly out to Manila, I developed an acute urinary infection. Rather than going to a doctor, I opted to continue our journey as planned and get treated there. We gave up our lovely hotel room and headed for the airport.

"There is a controllers' strike in Manila. No planes will be proceeding there today," the ticket attendant informed us. By then I was in quite a bit of pain and we had no place to stay – all hotels being booked. An agent at the airport managed to make arrangements for a room in the YMCA – plain, but clean and serviceable. My husband tucked me into bed, kissed me good-bye, and set off to find a doctor. Would he ever find his way back?

Much to my relief he did – with news of a nearby hospital where he was encouraged to bring me for an examination. When we arrived we were directed into a large waiting room furnished with rows of benches occupied by waiting patients. To my chagrin, as an American visitor, I was ushered in ahead of them. A diagnosis was made and medicine given. Being a socialistic medical system, no money was accepted in return for the service. Next day the strike was over and we made our way to Manila and the loving care of my sister-in-law, Rose Marie.

She immediately took a short walk across the yard to their neighbor who was a doctor and came back with a prescription for the medicine the hospital had given me. Jerry went and got it filled. It was wonderful being near family in this faraway place. That night, as we sat around the dinner table, we got into a discussion about smoking. Jerry, who was trying to give it up, found it hard to believe that I had never tried it. He began to have a strong urge to light up. Handing his 10-year-old son some coins he said, "Go up to the corner store and get me two cigarettes." He paused, then looking at me he added, "Get your aunt one, too." I tried it, but was more impressed by this strange land where cigarettes could be purchased singly by a child and medicine prescribed by a friendly neighbor.

After a few days I felt well enough to visit some of Jerry's parishioners in their small stilt houses. Jerry is a tall man – six foot four, but even I – five foot four, loomed high above these tiny people. From there we toured the rice fields terraced on high slopes near Bontoc. American naval officers who spent their R & R in that wild remote area nicknamed it the boondocks.

It had all been exciting. Yet scent of more adventure drew us to the lips of Taal, an active volcano on a nearby island – an island within an island.

"It's too dangerous," I insisted.

"What'll happen to our kids if we all blow up?" said Rose Marie.

But the guys would not be put off. Programmed from our girlhood that the man of the house makes the decisions, we went along. A young boatman, ready to risk his life for a few pesos, took us across the choppy water in his small outrigger –

named appropriately for our situation, La Bomba, meaning thrust. With a grin he explained to Jerry in Tagolog, that the word was commonly used in reference to sex films. Once across we headed toward the crater – up a hot black sandy slope amid tall tufts of yellow grass waving in the wind. About halfway up we heard the crater rumble and steam rose from the spot threatening activity. A quick look over the rim, just long enough to snap a picture of hot steaming fumaroles, convinced us it was time to turn back. Tired Rose Marie hitched a ride on her husband's back. Later we learned that vulcanologists had abandoned the site a day before we got there. Too dangerous.

    Back down unscathed, we settled in once more to quiet living – thankful to be alive – wondering why we'd been such fools.

SOUTH TO KERALA

It started on the plane from Malaysia to Madras – the pressure of people – body contact with strangers in a crowded aisle. The white-haired man in an impeccably white dhoti and shift, in the seat beside me, crowding me and forcing me to curl into myself. The crowds of young men, following us, haggling to carry our luggage the few short yards to customs and a waiting cab. The wild taxi ride, clutching my seat, craning my neck to watch my satchel tied precariously to the bumper. Being jolted to a stop at the first service station and forced to pay the fare prematurely, in order to buy enough gas to get us to the hotel. Now past the river where crowds of people were bathing and washing their clothes. On through this place where people press you as you walk, sleep in doorways inset from the street, and make their homes beneath the rising ramp of road, exposed to passersby. Leaving a trail of dust behind, we turned into the gardened entrance of the hotel. Looking out the window of our elegant room, I peered into the yard below and saw a tethered goat. India was the boyhood home of my husband and he was thoroughly enjoying every sight, sound, and smell. But I was afraid.

It didn't matter to me that they served poppadums with pepper flakes for dinner that night. Poppadums are large wafers made from rice or peas, somewhat like a tortilla. When dipped in hot oil they expand into crispy, crunchy morsels, like giant potato chips. Curry and poppadums were familiar favorites with me and I began to relax. "These are typical of the Tamils," my husband informed me – not his preference. But we both enjoyed the demonstration of temple dancing by a young woman, clothed in soft golden material that glowed as it swirled to her movements. The bright gold patches on her forehead and nose seemed exotic, and reminded me that I was far from home.

At the time we visited India tourists wishing to rent a car were required to hire a driver as well. We did so the next day. On our drive we passed a bullock cart loaded to overflowing with hay. "Why do they paint the bullock's horns red?" I asked my husband. "Indians love to decorate. They work so closely with their animals that they become like pets," he replied. Not too different from the rhinestone collars and bows we bestow on ours.

We were heading to Kanchipuram – one of India's seven Holy Cities – the city of 1,000 temples. At least one hundred twenty-four of them are extant. Not hard to miss the Ekambakeswara Temple, rising before us with its 188 foot Gupurum or tiered tower. It is one of the more recent temples – 16th century – possibly the largest. Dedicated to Shiva, its facades are decorated with intricate stone carvings. For all their beauty and excellence, I was most impressed by the temple, bathing ghat – a large open area in the inner court, filled with water. Steps, the width of one end, allow worshipers to enter the pool, bathe, wash their mundus (skirt-like cloth wraps), spread them on the steps to dry, and spend a quiet time sitting still and meditating. The bathers seemed at one with nature – oblivious to the others. So different from our crabbed bathrooms where we close and lock the door – hide ourselves from the world around us.

Before entering the inner temple we were required to remove our shoes. Two smiling boys provided us with slippers and the promise of "watching" our shoes. Redemption came with a few small coins.

Next we visited Kailasanatha Temple, built in the 8th century – one of the first dedicated to Siva. Varaddajaswamy Temple is noted for its exquisite stone carvings and its Hall of Pillars. It was dedicated to Vishnu in the 16th century. Tucked in here and there are intricate erotic carvings. In the temple courtyard a Brahmin priest directed the temple elephant to bless me by touching my head lightly with its trunk. The 8th century Vaikuntha Perumal Temple is one of the few that bars non-Hindus from the sanctuary. Its carvings chiefly depict the wars of the ancient Pallava dynasty. From the rooftop we had a fantastic view of our surroundings.

In a village, on the way back to the hotel, we passed an Indian Coffee House. A simple, open fronted structure, where the locals were enjoying their cup of brew, much as we at Starbucks. Moving on we passed a field of water, where young women, with their colorful saris tucked up above their knees, stooped and planted stalks of rice.

We took the train next day to my husband's birthplace, at the southern tip of the country. Police in stiff, pointed khaki shorts stood guard at the stations. Men clad in mundus mustered near the track, armed with shovels and picks. Monkeys perched on nearby roofs. And there were people. People with black parasols. And people. People and people and palms. Swaying palms. Coconut palms. Forests of palms like forests of pines. Backwaters lapped at their feet. And women in saris. Black shining hair. Clean shining hair. Sweeping their yards with a broom. And pink and green houses. Men tedding hay. Barefoot children waving good-day. Bananas and rice fields and streams. Chenganoor, Trichur, Quilon, Trivandrum. Kerala. Garden of India: home.

Our first stop, Trivandrum, the capital of Kerala, introduced me to a touch of the life my father-in-law experienced in his twenty-five years as a missionary in India. We stopped at the school where he had first served while learning the Malayalam language. The headmaster introduced us to the children. With wide smiles they cheered, waved, and sang for us. We completely disrupted their day.

We visited the lovely veranda'd house of my husband's childhood on the compound near Nilamel, a small village outside the city of Trivandrum. The house looked the same to my husband, but was being used now as a kindergarten. The second house that had been situated on the compound had been mined for material to build a school. As we drove west toward Quilon, he noted other changes. An area that had once been fields of rice, was now covered with roadside shops. He noted, too, a sharp rise in population. The white saris, once worn exclusively by the Malayalam women had been exchanged for brightly colored cloth. Since water is plentiful in that area, the white he remembered sparkled like the clean black tresses of their hair. My western clothes, which exposed my legs, were a disturbing attraction. Often when we stopped, men came up to the car window on my side and looked me up and down. I vowed, if I ever came again, I would wear long skirts. We had a pleasant stop for lunch with our driver who knew where to find good curry and dhal. Large rectangular concrete sinks with running water are furnished in the dining areas of many restaurants, to insure clean hands – before and after eating – for the Indian's habit of balling up the rice with their fingers and dipping it into the curry.

Making a circle back toward Trivandrum we saw groups of women along the backwater canals, washing their clothes and spreading them to dry atop varlaams pulled near to the shore. Varlaams are simple canoe-like boats with dome shaped coverings of coconut mats. They are used to carry freight along the canals that connect to backwater routes. Further on we came to Varkala where red cliffs and bucolic beach scenes lined the coast. We stopped to take a picture of the Mission Hospital and Dispensary, which my father-in-law used when he ran the boarding school at nearby Nilamel. The place was well maintained, but Dr. Samuel, of my husband's fond memory, was no longer with them.

Trivandrum itself is a fascinating city to visit. Government buildings such as the museum, library, Zoological Park entrance gates, and general communications, are well kept up and built in a lovely style unique to that city – spired windows, towers with peaked or domed roofs, red brick walls – some with intermittent rows of decorated tiles. Palms and dense greenery are everywhere. We caught a glimpse of the tri-spired, red tiled roof of a palace, peeking out from behind an earthen wall – once the home of the Maharajah of Travancore (Kerala's former name). But the main attraction for my husband was the sidewalk shop across the street from the Mascot Hotel where we stayed. There he found the small Kerala bananas remembered from his childhood.

Padmanabhaswami Temple – the city's main landmark is dedicated to Vishnu. Only Hindus are allowed inside. The tiered facade of the wide Gupurum is covered with intricate carvings. As we stood in awe, a holy man who spent his time begging at the temple approached us. He had a long scraggly beard and wore a rusty orange turban with shirt and mundu to match. In his hand he carried a wooden begging bowl and a bamboo walking stick.

A short drive out to the seaside at Kovalam brought us to a pristine beach and cove, back-dropped by forests of coconut palms. A beach house is still provided up beyond the sand for locals, but a luxurious hotel now rises in the background. We visited several of the mission compounds in the environs – each with its so-called bungalow – lovely, sprawling stone houses with tiled roofs and large breezy verandas.

Spencer's – in the heart of Trivandrum was a must. Here my husband had accompanied his father on shopping sprees for items imported from England – treats such as ham, sausage, syrups, and jams. Spencer's, I was told, has everything. In our travels I had stopped at numerous roadside shops and asked for curry powder. No one seemed to understand until – at one place a smiling man proudly produced a can of talcum powder from his shelf. But true to its reputation, Spencer's carried tins of Quilon curry powder. In wondering aloud why this British store would carry an Indian item while the local shops did not, I was informed that the Indians don't rely on canned goods – they make their own curry paste – fresh each day – crushing the leaves with a mortar and pestle.

Next day, we headed south toward Neyoor, to the tiny hospital near the doctor's bungalow where my husband was born. On our drive we saw mounds of rice spread to dry along the road. Crossing vehicles would break the husks in readiness for winnowing. In nearby brown-watered ponds men and oxen bathed as one. At the hospital we found people in the yard, squatting over small charcoal burners, preparing food for their sick family members.

"The patients get well quicker if their families take care of them and feed them what they are used to eating," said the nurse, taking us through the primitive wards.

We continued south, to the tip of the continent, Kanyakumari or Cape Comorin – a holy place where small temples line the shore and a monument to Gandhi presides. Blue, blue water, as I had seen it in my dreams, but so crowded with market stands and monuments that there was but one bare plot of beach where I could go down to the water's edge to tip my toe and touch the tongue of the bottom of the world.

We headed north to the hill station in Kodaikanal, where my husband had attended boarding school. We drove all day through hot and dusty plains, palm strewn cities, raucous, odoriferous bazaars, roads teeming with beasts and bikes, buses, lorries, and loaded bullock carts.

Up and over precarious, winding mountain passes where sparse, slender palms played lookout for tender chaparral and green chenille-spread tea bushes covered rolling hills. Down into dry, dusty desert roads lined with dusty men, we dodged cattle, goats and wagonloads of hay.

The promised lunch stop turned out to be a couple warm beers from a roadside shop and the restroom was a path to a ditch under the shelter of a tree. By the time we turned onto the Ghat Road, which was the last steep climb, we were already several hours late. This might be home to my husband, but I was exhausted and overwrought.

Around a bend, past a white washed post, signifying Anglo-land, the rented car broke down. Unperturbed, Ahmed, our driver, left us by the roadside under tall tamarind trees while he hitched a ride back to the nearest town for help. We were not far from a small village, and since it was late afternoon people kept passing by, driving their herds of goats as they headed home. One withered, old woman with scraggly hair and no teeth latched herself onto us. She followed me around and around the car, staring and trying to communicate.

"Don't give to people out in the open," my husband had warned me. "You'll be inundated."

But skin-deep, sculptured bones and caverned eyes unarmed me. I yearned to give. This woman's insistent stares disturbed me and I tried to persuade my husband to give her some money, hoping then she would go away.

"She doesn't want money," he replied. "She's just curious."

Eventually she got bored and went on down the road. She was soon replaced by a professional beggar. Upon seeing us in our predicament, he stopped, pulled a tattered piece of cloth from his sack and carefully draped it around his shoulders. He, too, followed me from one side of the car to the other as I tried to escape his stares.

Finally I climbed inside the car and pulled my hat down over my eyes, hoping to discourage him. But that only made him try harder. He stood next to my window and began making loud sobbing noises.

At this point I became completely unnerved. "Give him some money," I screamed at my husband.

"Pordah! Be off!" he said, giving the man some coins.

"What were you afraid of?" he asked. "You saw for yourself it was all an act."

By then another group of people was approaching. My husband raised his hand and smiled in greeting, "Salaam, salaam."

Oh don't do that, I thought. Let well enough alone.

I began to feel ashamed however, as they came over to the car to see what was wrong and try to help. Like actors, they conveyed their sympathy with gestures and expressions, even offering to go back to the village to get coconut milk for us to drink. I began to relax amid the salaams and smiles as they proceeded on their way. But when the chicken, which had been hanging from their bike, lifted its head with a loud "squawk!" – I must have jumped a foot.

Finally a car pulled up with our driver. A crowd of onlookers piled out with him and watched as he deftly exchanged the broken part with one he had scrounged off another Ambassador back in the town. Soon after we were on our way.

As I sat safe and settled later in our hotel room, the dark, sooty-suited man laying a fire in the fireplace, dispelled the damp and gloom – more with his gilded smile, than with his sticks in trade. Of what and whom was I afraid?

NUTRITION – INSPIRATION

"A ROSE IS A ROSE IS A ROSE"

"What do you think it's right to pray for?" my friend asked.

"I'm in a hurry," I said. "I'll think about it and talk to you on Wednesday." I sounded like I knew. But I was still trying to decipher phrases like "A rose is a rose is a rose," in the poetry class we were attending. How could I answer such a question?

Perhaps there is no single answer. Maybe the question itself, shows a lack of understanding about prayer, for prayer is more than a scribbled shopping list or a child's letter to Santa. Prayer has often been described as conversation with God, with everything that true conversation entails, including both speaking and listening. At best it begins with an awe-filled awareness or hope that God is attuned to our specific wavelength.

We do not start out our lives knowing how to converse. Perhaps, like a rose, prayers go through stages in their development – first a shoot, then a hard knob upon the stalk, then leaves, a bud, a gradual awakening of the bloom, and a final fade before the fall.

If you happened to start with a Germanic background like mine, you probably began your prayer life with a few simple words such as, "Abba Vater, Amen." When we are young we call on Dad if we are frightened; and so we also pray, "keep me safe till morning bright."

Later we begin to ask for specific things, and because Dad loves us, he gives us the bike or Barbie doll we want. I call this the "gimme" period, like the time I was young and desperate, standing at the corner of Bonanza and Diablo, waiting for the Greyhound Bus. I needed to meet my fiancé in the city, fifteen miles away, to get the blood tests for our upcoming wedding. The invitations were all out. I could almost smell the cake. This was my last chance. As I waited I grew frantic and prayed. "Please God, help me get – gimme – a ride." A nice, safe looking, woman drove up to the stop sign, ready to turn right. Then she called to me, "Going into Oakland? Come on. Hop in. I'll give you a lift. These buses aren't always reliable."

That worked pretty well; and so one begins to ask for more "things." Dad says, "Well, maybe. But you know, your mother needs a new washer and your sister needs braces." We begin to see that our little wants don't count for much and we feel foolish now to ask. We realize that God has many children, with a multitude of needs. We begin to see that asking God to make the day sunny for our picnic might deprive farmers of their needed rain.

Now the leaves shoot out. We look around and notice other people's problems. Perhaps your prayer, like mine, is for assistance in finding a helper for an aging mother. The focus shifts to fitting needs and goals together – no more "my sunshine versus the farmer's rain."

The bud is forming. We struggle to understand how it all works out, and so we cry out, "Lord I believe; help thou mine unbelief" (Mark 9:24 KJV). And an answer comes – maybe through a friend, or a sermon we are sure was ear-marked just for us, or perhaps, (as has happened many times to me) through daily Scripture reading.

And like a rose, we finally bloom. We ask God to help us blossom full and bright, to make a lovely scent for some sick, despairing soul to savor, that they may turn their eyes to the Rose of Sharon and his message that God loves us.

And then, like a fading rose that drops its petals in old age, we return once more to our beginnings, and know it is all right to simply say, "Abba, Father, Amen."

BACK FROM THE BRINK

"Leave his bag in your car," the registrar told us. "Until you know which room he'll be assigned to."

My husband was entering the hospital for a standard surgical procedure. It was expected to take a couple of hours and require no more than two nights stay.

I kissed him good-bye at the entrance to surgery at 5:30, Thursday morning. The attendant directed me to wait in the family room of the outpatient division where I ran into a woman from our neighborhood. We exchanged our reasons for being there – surgeries for her son and for my husband.

The day wore on and on and still no word. I was glad for my neighbor's presence and her help in passing the time, but my concern was growing. What happened? What went wrong? At last I approached the volunteer. She called surgery and was told I should expect a several hour delay. By that time my neighbor's son was released. "I'll pray for your husband," she said as she waved good-bye.

Pray. Yes. That's what I need to do, I thought. But maybe he wouldn't want me to. I was thinking of all those heated discussions we had had concerning prayer. I was a long time believer that God often gives us what we ask for. Perhaps – just because we acknowledge him and ask. My husband disagreed. "What about those other people who pray and don't get what they ask for?" he would counter. I was well aware that it wasn't something magic. It had been my experience that sometimes God says yes. Sometimes he says no – but gives us grace to cope. And sometimes he says wait. His words had set me wondering, but I began to pray.

Late that afternoon the doctors finally appeared with their report, wearing weary, worried looks. Once they'd gotten inside his body, they found a nest of complications. My husband was critically ill. His lungs were damaged and he needed to be on a respirator. "He'll have to stay in recovery for a while," they said. "Then they'll send him to CCU and let you know when you can see him."

So I waited and prayed some more. It was time now, too, for the volunteer at the desk to go home. She instructed me to stay there and answer her phone when they called. Time went on and on until I became frantic. I found my way to CCU and entered – without the regulation tag. When a young male nurse approached and asked how he could help, I burst into tears. "I said goodbye to my husband early this morning and I don't know where he is or how he is." He sat me down and after some phone calls, informed me that my husband would be there soon.

As I waited in the nearby family room, I finally saw that beloved face being wheeled through the corridor. After getting him settled, they called me in – warning me to prepare for a shock. Tubes were in his nose and mouth, a respirator pulsed nearby, drainage tubes were connected to plastic containers lining the wall behind him, a screen beeped, flashing signs of his vitals. I was overwhelmed and asked if I could stay the night. They were very kind, but said, "No."

That was bad enough, but by the next weekend I watched the nurse struggle to bring his vital signs up. The doctor was called in and told me, "He has multi-system organ failure. His only hope is another operation, but I doubt he can make it through alive." His words struck like a lightning bolt – leaving a big black hole in my heart. No! No! I don't want to lose him yet, I screamed inside. After fifty-three years of marriage one begins to take a relationship for granted, but that night I knew without a doubt, how much I cared for him.

I called our children – 3,000 miles away – and prayed. Our friend, Jon, came and stood by me as they prepared for the operation. "With all these machines and tubes, I can't even reach to kiss him good-bye," I said. "Don't worry," the nurse said. "We'll fix it so you can." When everything had been unplugged from the wall and realigned into a battery at the foot of the bed, we were able to reach him. Jon took my husband's hand and told him he'd never had such a wonderful friend. I kissed him once for each of our four children, naming them as I did. Then I kissed him from myself – thanking him for being such a good husband. There was no sign that he had heard. I went to the family room sobbing uncontrollably. When the doctor came with his report, the smile on his face, told us there was hope.

I notified my husband's siblings and friends, who all began to pray for him. Our children came, and even the scoffers among them, prayed. The ensuing week added the dialysis machine to his plastic life. At least he was still living and we had hope. Until the weekend rolled around again – bringing news that the sack around his heart was filling with fluid. Another surgery, another life threatening situation, from which they didn't expect him to survive.

Everyone who heard about it prayed for him. The maid who cleaned his room. The nurses and the doctors. Our family and friends. People who waited in the Family Room for news of their own loved ones. The pastor who came to call. The nuns as they made their rounds. As they rolled the gurney down the hall toward surgery, I ran up, asking if I could kiss him. "We don't have time," they called as they rushed on.

But once again I saw the gurney return with my husband's living body. While they had him out on the operating table, they performed a tracheotomy so the tubes could be removed from his mouth and oxygen could be transmitted through the opening in his throat. At least he was more comfortable.

"How is your husband?" people asked. "We're praying for him."

I assumed they were praying that he'd get well. But it seemed that every time we thought he was recovering, some major set back appeared. At last – instead of asking God to heal him – I put it in his hands. "Dear God," I said. "I don't know which way to pray – what to ask for. You know all things, so you know he wouldn't want to be kept alive on machines. Please do what you think best and help me cope."

Slowly his condition improved. The dialysis machine was put aside, the oxygen supply was weaned, tubes were taken out, needles removed. After six weeks he was moved to intermediate care and then to rehab. Two months from the day I took him there, I brought him home. A man alive.

CATCHING THE RING

"Pack up your troubles in an old kit bag – and smile, smile, smile." So goes an old song. We recognize the foolishness of a Pollyanna philosophy, yet we cling to it as a child to his mother's skirt. Believers have been mocked for centuries for fleeing earth's monsters and seeking entrance into Eden through God's Mercy Shuttle. Though a virus may not be immune to cure – a cure may become immune. So it is we ever seek new hatches for escape.

Common sense tells us it is smart to be prepared. They say if NASA had prepared a proper emergency landing for the Challenger, the astronauts and teacher might have survived the accident. But does preparation always work?

Tourist agencies tout packaged "Sea Escapes" or flights to far off lands where one ends up bumping into his own neighbor or his clone. Others pack up their Granola in their blue backpacks and head for the Sierra trails where bears must yield to traffic and ears are pierced with boom box blasts.

As a child I grew used to my mother's verbalized wish that she could take our family to a South Pacific island and bypass the impending war. How was she to know the war would be fought there? In spite of civil rights, how many people haven't left their comfortable, paid for homes, in order to flee from dark complexioned neighbors or crime infested spots, only to find they have been followed.

That white Bengal tiger at the Miami Metro Zoo might have lost his stripes, but he's a tiger just the same. We often try to bleach out spots of misery only to find we've caused a tear.

There comes a time we need to realize pacifiers seldom work. We're only sucking air if we think we can side-step trouble or our fears. I learned that from my Peeping Tom.

Our house was a brown-shingled Swiss chalet – covered with ivy. Sitting in the living room and reading, I'd hear strange noises. I heard it more when I was alone and had the children bedded down. Was someone there?

Each night I tried to convince myself it was just the wind scraping the ivy against the stained glass piano window on the porch side outer wall. But why did I feel compelled to call, "Scram," when I opened the back door? Why did I sweep the crumbs from beneath the supper table no further than the door stoop? Why did those crumbs look stepped on in the morning? And why did four year old Diana take her bubble gum, as I read to the children from the Wizard of Oz, and plug the keyhole shut? Surely we all felt someone lurking there.

Lot's wife – I sat one night – turned to a pillar of fright, unable to ignore sounds of feet instead of leaves. I never turned a page – only strained to listen. I heard the click, click of traffic as it passed across a foil plate out on the street. When my husband pulled over it to park, the sound of running footsteps on the wooden porch was unmistakable. When we looked over the railing, our visitor ran down the sidewalk, jumped the hedge and fled. At last, after several more incidents, I convinced my husband we should move. Eventually we did.

A nice – two-storied house – where I could view the porch from up above.

A nice – two-storied house – with a history of murder.

A nice – two-storied house – with a doorbell ringing late one stormy night – when I was all alone.

Around and around we go on the carousel of life – trying to catch the ring. A roseola virus – measled escapism follows man through lifetimes – each generation choosing its own vaccine. Since the choice is mine to make, I think I'll stick to God's Mercy Shuttle.

I like its aura of adventure, of mystery, and hope. It has a catchy ring.

MAKING BABIES

"The petty cash had babies again," I said to the other bookkeepers. My monthly accounting overage had become an in-house office joke. I was glad not to be short, but it bothered me to be over. Had I cheated someone making change?

A few days later I was struck by a headline in the *Miami Herald*: HATE CRIMES INCREASE. Earlier articles reported an increase in crime. Now it had become "hate" crime. Crime was having babies, too.

Some time after, I watched a panel on CNN discuss the upsurge of killings by youth. Not gang related strangers, but people they knew or were acquainted with from school. The panelists came up with several reasons: availability of guns, lack of parental discipline, TV news coverage, TV shows and games, childhood abuse. Their analysis seemed plausible, yet someone pointed out that many children with the same influences were not affected negatively. I began to wonder – was *hate* involved here, too?

Does the cause lie deeper than guns or television? Perhaps there is a seed lying dormant within us that, penetrated by some real or imagined hurt, is fertilized by anger. We let it grow, mulling the offense over and over in our minds until it is attached. Cells divide and multiply into a fetus of hate. We feed and nurture it with prenatal care – telling ourselves that what Dick, or Jane, or Jamie did is unforgivable. Next we add some vitamins – comments that increase our hate. "I could kill that guy." "That dirty so and so deserves to die." "String him up." The organism grows inside and misshapes us. Our voice takes on a mean tone. Our face a snarling look. Our appetite increases. We need more gory details to feed our growing monster.

Too late for an abortion, we end up giving birth to hate in lethal, subtle acts of revenge. The recipient is penetrated. The cycle is renewed. Another babe of hate is born. Wouldn't it be great if we could take a pill to prevent its inception? How <u>can</u> we curb this population explosion?

I remember my own youth. Going to Sunday school. Hearing the words, "Love others as yourself. Love your enemies. Forgive. Forgive as God forgives." I remember learning what that means – watching my parents kiss and make up when Dad stayed out too late playing poker with the boys. Or when he danced too close with that woman – Flossy.

How wonderful to be free from that burden in our belly. As any mother knows, labor pains hurt. It's hard to forgive. Yet if we fail to forgive we find ourselves full and ripe with hate. Ready to deliver. It's the way of the world. Everything has babies.

MOTHERING WORKS

"Tell them it's not easy," my daughter said when I told her I was writing an article in defense of working mothers.

Added to the mental and physical stress of juggling two jobs, working mothers often find themselves burdened by snide and insinuating remarks from people in the surrounding society – judgments that reaffirm their confusion about the rightness of their choice to work outside the home. It is not only uncertainty they feel, but pain and guilt as well. Many young women think they are lacking in true motherhood by their part-time mothering. They envy the stay-at-home position their mothers enjoyed. They ache for that special bonding that comes between a child and its mother. "Mom stayed home with us," they say in worried tones.

Young parents today have different situations to deal with than Mom did. For most, the option of staying home with their children never even enters the picture. Ten fingers and ten toes do not provide enough digits to add up the formidable cost of rent or mortgage payments. It is not always choice that draws young mothers to the market, but the pig they need to bring home jiggedy-jig, so they can feed their families.

Grandmothers, aunts, teachers, fathers, god-mothers, grandfathers – even neighbors on the block – have often been on the scene to help parents raise their children. Think how many "nannies" there must have been in King Solomon's palace. Royalty and wealthy people have traditionally left the raising of their children to ayahs, servant girls, and nursemaids. Sarah, the mother of the Judeo-Christian culture, had a handmaiden's help.

The African American families of our country, torn apart by traders, then by economics, were not allowed to develop in the traditional manner. Instead of being limited to a part-time mother, they often had to deal with the lack of a father figure as well. Yet they managed to raise fine children.

In the mountains of Guatemala, where Day Cares don't exist, tiny women – backs bent beneath large loads of firewood – carry young children in their shawls slung across their breasts. These children end up weak and atrophied from lack of exercise. Nearness does not automatically spell – best.

Whether the modern woman is forced out of the home for financial reasons or chooses to pursue a career, there are many ways in which she can carry out her commitment to be a good mother. She can compensate for being away by making evenings, weekends, and vacations prime time hours with her children. Helping children with their homework naturally falls in the after dinner hour, whether one is a stay-at-home mother or not.

Engaging her husband to help with the household chores (if she can manage that trick) will free her for more time with the children. Or she can involve the children in systematic routines, doing these chores together. This in turn makes them feel important, needed, and loved.

Care can be taken in choosing just the "right person or day care," for the children. Time can be spent attending religious services with them and introducing them to the spiritual side of their lives. Doing without some material things and using the money to provide for after school supervision can also prove to be an act of good mothering. The children will not be young for long. They will soon be on their own. Time enough then for that special "thing" mother wants.

Planning ahead for meals is another important aspect of mothering. Too tired when they get home from work to stop and prepare a healthy meal, many women end up rustling the family into line at a fast food place, filling them up on fried foods, and using half that extra money the job was meant to provide. Fresh vegetables can be cleaned and stored in the refrigerator for the week, on Saturday. The kids can help with that. Meals do not have to be elaborate or gourmet. The important thing is to plan ahead. Few women have the strength to plan by the time they come home from work, but they can have cans and packages lined up on the shelf – ready to open and tuck into the microwave. Who says you have to start from scratch like Mom did?

Then, instead of the evening news, let the hour be spent together at the supper table, listening to each other's days, healing each other's wounds, bringing perspective into the day's joys and problems. It's like an old game on a new board. But there is nothing new about the players. They can still touch base by surrounding their home life and children with moves of love, proving in their own way that it is not the hours we bring to mothering that count. It is the commitment. Mothering works.

SUBMIT? TO MY HUSBAND?

"I'm never going to get married and have some guy tell me what to do," my daughter said.

One husband and two kids later she doesn't even remember saying that. Was it she that changed or has the idea of submission to husbands been left, like some abandoned farmhouse, to crumble and decay?

Middle-aged women today, trying to advise their daughters, find themselves in a precarious position straddling the divide that question posits. One foot remains on the side of old traditions where they watched their grandmother's unquestioning obedience, felt their mothers begin to chafe, and experienced their own emerging rebellious stance. The other stretches toward the side of a new era via ERA and NOW where daughters claim their rights for equal pay and benefits, demand freedom from sexual harassment and abuse, and expect domestic help from husbands.

But are women less in bondage to diaper bags and Day Care, time clocks and bosses' glowers, than tied to the rise and fall of seasons and sun – home beside the range? Does the trouble lie in the *word* submit or our interpretation of it?

As I see my daughter now, happily married, I wonder – did she change her mind and get married because she learned to submit to a man? Or did she finally catch on that submission is an act of love?

I'm not sure how that came about. Let's just say I've noticed each of them submitting. Both love to cook and sometimes she submits and lets him fix the meal and sometimes, when she offers to clean up, I see him submitting, too.

THE ART OF RECEIVING

"Clank," the quarter rolled across the floor. Dad's boss had accidentally pulled it out of his pocket. I quickly ran and brought it back to him.

"You keep it," he said as he smiled at me.

"Oh, no!" I exclaimed. A whole quarter? I couldn't take all that money.

His smile turned to a frown as he gruffly replied, "Never forget this, young lady: When someone wants to give you something, don't refuse it."

I was somehow confused and disappointed. Instead of being grateful to me, he was a bit angry. I have often thought since then, as I heard people arguing over who would pay the bill, refusing to accept help in time of need, or rejecting someone's offer of a gift, that sometimes we do need lessons in receiving. Several examples come to my mind, which demonstrate the kinds of things we are often called upon to receive and why we should do so.

For instance, at one time I suddenly became seriously ill and had to have major surgery. My husband has a good job and income and could well afford to pay for help. But our neighbors are loving people and genuinely wanted to show their concern. My husband wisely accepted one neighbor's offer to iron his shirts. I really think she was hurt the next week when I felt well enough to arrange for the laundry to do it. I had denied her the pleasure of being helpful.

Who hasn't heard some well-meaning parents tell their children, "Now don't go getting something for us for Christmas. We've got everything we need." Those children love and appreciate their parents. They want to express that love in a tangible way.

Or what about my daughter-in-law's aunt who lives near- by? She has no means of transportation and few friends because she is new in the area. I took her to lunch one day and afterwards she invited me in. She had a new blouse which she realized did not fit her properly. She wanted me to have it. Then I remembered the scene in my childhood home. Why not take it and let her say thanks? After all, she's not the poor relation. Why make her feel like she is?

My mother has a friend who, somewhere in her life, learned the art of receiving. She is retired and has a substantial pension. She is the only one of her group of friends who still drives. When the ladies gratefully slip her some money to help pay for the gas she uses when she drives them places, she turns around and gives it to some charity. What better way to give the ladies a feeling of independence?

For years when I visited my mother who lives in another state, she kept saying, "I want to take you to The Train Station for dinner. You'll just love it." "Some day," I would reply unenthusiastically. I'd been around the world and too many Train Stations.

Then one day her insistence prevailed and I found it was indeed a unique restaurant. On top of that we had a pleasant adventure taking her local mini-bus to our destination, enabling me to see first-hand how well she manages to get around. We dined in style in the beautiful, wood paneled, private Pullman car. You could almost hear her thoughts: "See, I'm not just a dumb old lady. I'm an individual with something new to show you."

Why had I waited so long to receive?

THE FELLOWSHIP OF WOMEN

We were on a safari in Africa and had interrupted our afternoon game drive to visit a Samburu tribal village just outside the Samburu Game Reserve in Kenya. After negotiating with the chief for permission, my husband busied himself taking pictures. I suddenly found myself closely surrounded by the women, whose eyes unabashedly explored me up and down. They felt my skirt, examined my hat and belt, and touched my skin. They knew enough English to get across the usual questions: Name? Babies? Girls? Boys? After several days of little exercise and lots of eating, my stomach was beginning to show the effects. Much to my chagrin the women poked my belly and asked, "Baby?" One woman kept tugging at me saying, "See house." Their uninhibited intimacy caused me to reflect again on a phenomenon I call the Fellowship of Women.

Traveling through some of the more primitive parts of the world, I have often noted a community among the women. They share the tedious tasks of subsistence: planting rice, cultivating crops, carrying loads of firewood up steep mountain paths. I have seen them gathered together at the watering places: community wells, taps, river and lakes. I have seen them laughing and have heard their chatter as they bathe, wash their clothes, and fill their water pots. Their colorful markets line the streets and roadways of the world. In their simple homes there is often a widowed grandmother or other unmarried woman.

In the more developed countries we do not have this kind of community. We move to big cities and isolate ourselves within our nuclear families. Few of us even know our next-door neighbors. Our relatives are thousands of miles away. With modern appliances we do our household chores alone or relate only to a machine in an office.

But no matter how sophisticated we become, the basic need of women to share their experiences always becomes apparent. Get two or three women together and before long they are exchanging notes on children or swapping recipes. Show us a baby – be it animal or human – and hear us ooh and aah. I have a friend who lives three thousand miles away from me. Occasionally we call each other and often end up laughing at ourselves for spending a long distance call talking weather or recipes. The first time I returned to California after moving to Florida, the satisfaction I felt at seeing the mountains again was comparable to a drink of cold water after a long, dusty ride. I get the same feeling from a good talk fest with my mother or one of our daughters after a reunion.

Could it be that unhappiness in marriage and the rise in alcoholism among women stem, in part, from a lack of female community? What our sisters before us enjoyed with each other, we now project onto our husbands. But men don't enjoy female chitchat. "You never talk to me," is a frequently heard dirge. It is not an unworthy cry, but we expect too much of men if we want them to fill our need for feminine community. We are asking them to be our sisters as well as our husbands. When they can't or won't, many seek relief in a new man or perhaps a bottle.

Being aware that we have given up something vital for our modern way of life may help us cope. Instead of floundering helplessly, burdening our husbands, or refusing to become "joiners," we might accept the idea that we need a trade-off. Perhaps the feminists are reacting to a survival instinct when they ask women of this country to rally to their cause. The ERA with its simple call for equality of rights under the law is a commendable rallying point. There are many more: flower clubs, book clubs, League of Women Voters, PTA, NOW, hospital auxiliaries, church societies, a job – the list can go on and on.

It is not hard to see that women's groups not only provide much needed fellowship, but often offer it in an environment of love and growth, learning and service. Whatever our interest, we modern women can find relief and satisfaction for the gnawing, empty pit produced by isolation and recapture a place in the Fellowship of Women.

THIS I BELIEVE

Born in a small Dakota prairie town, I was taken to the church a few days later, to be baptized into the Christian faith. My childhood was spent in the womb-like setting of loving parents, family, and church who taught me to believe in God. As I grew they also taught me what to believe ABOUT God. Time went on and I found myself straining against doubts about creedal dogmas, as though I were shutting my eyes and gritting my teeth saying, "I believe – I believe – I believe!

Nevertheless, I tried to follow the tenets of our church as they applied to all aspects of life, such as, choice of mate, raising children, and how I used my time. A lot of it was spent trying to get a children's script I wrote aired on TV as an outreach program – thinking God had led me to do it. I had been fighting my doubts all along, but the failure of that project finally reached me. Perhaps I was wrong about God. That – and the emptiness I felt from liturgy, rituals, and gilded robes – stirred me to look deeper. I started to read what theologians like Lewis, Kierkegaard, Spong, and others had to say. Delving into the Bible, especially the Gospels.

Eventually I dropped my church membership in an effort to get far away from childhood teachings and start anew. I visited other churches, prayed, and read more theology books. Through it all, I found there is one aspect of religion I could not deny. I felt that God had always heard my prayers. Sometimes he answered yes, sometimes wait, sometimes no – always helping me cope, no matter which answer came. He has been with me in spite of rules, robes, and rituals – tenets and creeds. And he is still here with me without them. It took me a lifetime to realize that following someone else's ideas about God, is just that – following – not belief. I believe that God is vastly beyond all man-made concepts of him, but like the small girl in the small Dakota town, I believe he's there.

UNSEEN POWER

Peace! Peace! Peace! becomes our chant as we daily view the horrors of war and hurts in our relationships. Wouldn't it be wonderful if we could find a magic formula to erase those hates and bring peace? Could we find a formula for global peace from our experiences with finding it in our close relationships? Think of the countless marriages which have been saved from breaking up by the power of forgiveness and reconciliation.

But what exactly do those words mean? According to the dictionary forgive means to pardon or overlook. It means being merciful or compassionate. Reconcile means to restore or bring back to friendship or union.

One friend of mine never allowed me to do that. She just refused to answer my calls and letters, so I never knew what I had done to destroy our friendship. I often wonder if I am still a sore spot moldering in her heart.

I am reminded of another friend who was offended by a letter I wrote to her. She replied that she forgave me for what I said, but no longer wanted to be my friend. I wrote back, told her I was sorry, and would like to continue our friendship. But she never did and I was devastated.

Another example comes to mind about a relative who did something very hurtful. I was able to forgive the person, but it was awkward at family get-togethers since no apology was given and socializing felt false. There was a terrible gap between us that couldn't be spanned with friendly posturing. After lengthy communications via letters and e-mail an "I'm sorry," arrived. I immediately felt reconciled.

Forgiveness is not easy. It is not magic. It takes more than an Open Sesame or an Abracadabra. It takes time. Like the time I was left with a huge hematoma over my left eye from a bad fall. First the blood drained into my eyes, turning them black (standing out like a raccoon's), and continuing down my face to my neck. People did a double take when seeing me – especially kids. My poor husband kept saying, "I didn't do it." Anger and hate can do this to us, too – discolor our souls. It took over three months for my face to heal. Perhaps our hurt will leave a permanent scar – like the loss of a loved one, but over time forgiveness, like wounds, heals.

Forgiveness goes beyond self. Early man learned to survive by destroying his enemies. That reaction has snowballed to the extent that the whole of mankind is threatened with extinction through modern weapons. If each individual would forgive his enemies, perhaps that reaction would snowball to the whole of mankind. For example, if married couples would openly forgive each other, their children would learn to do so from their example. This could work with siblings, parents, fellow workers, neighbors, etc., and snowballing could begin.

Forgiveness involves thought and effort. We need to discuss the situation with the one who did the hurting instead of letting if fester inside of us. We need to seek ways to resolve the problem. Globally that means peace talks and across the table discussions, face to face.

Forgiveness offers gifts. As my mother said when she referred to my dad's infidelity, "I really loved that man. What would life have been without him?"

Perhaps the idea of forgiveness – its meaning and application – is something mankind needs to explore and disseminate. Especially to children who are the ones who could start the snowball rolling.

Forgiveness also frees us from incarceration:

Self-destruct

Heavy hangs
the unforgiving heart –
draped in drab attire,
its fired red snuffed out.
Locked in self-perpetuating pout
eyes focus inward
and like internal bleeding

drain vesicles
of life imparting power.

Walking prison cells,
blocked from unbarred vision,
we fail to see
we free ourselves
when others are forgiven.

In THE PAINTED VEIL, when talking about Walter's inability or refusal to forgive his wife's infidelity, Somerset Maugham notes, "Was it not pitiful that men, tarrying so short a space in a world where there was so much pain, should thus torture themselves?"

FRAGRANCE – HUMOR

ALMOST THERE

"You must be crazy, Joe," Daddy's friends said, "six thousand miles in a Volkswagen mini-bus with four squabbling kids?"

Daddy grinned and scratched his head. It wouldn't be hard on him. Mart always let him sit in front. Neither of them felt obliged to talk. They could ride for hours without saying a word. Daddy never had to worry about which road to take – Mart studied maps and planned the routes.

As soon as school was out, summer 1962, we took to the road. California to Connecticut via the South. When we reached the intersection at the end of our block, Diana looked up. "Are we almost there?" We spent the first night in Barstow and the second in Phoenix. When we arrived in El Paso the third night, I went with Daddy to check out the motel room.

"It's just as seedy as those last two," I said.

"But it's cheap."

"Well – O.K. But I'm not cooking here."

We found a place nearby that served quick Texas Barbeque and walked across the bridge to explore Juarez. By the time we got back, my mind was whirring with pictures of people climbing the cathedral steps on their knees as ragged children begged for a coin. The motel didn't see so ratty anymore.

It took another two nights to get through Texas. Mama didn't mind how long it took. She was happy with the mini-bus and its fifty-mile an hour limit. She sat in back and kept the children entertained playing games. I took charge of the cooler, doling out celery sticks and carrot snacks. The official tour guide – making sure Mart stopped at everything important: pointing out cows, clouds, wild flowers and keeping a running inspection of the sky for signs of a tornado.

"Just look at those beautiful clouds."

No one ever did.

A major item on my agenda was Carlsbad Caverns. I hadn't reckoned with Mama's claustrophobia and was almost sorry we had come when I saw the look of fear on her face as we wended through the deep caves.

"It won't be so bad going up, Mama. We'll take the elevator."

That was even worse. Mama was sure her heart had stopped several hundred feet below.

At the top Mart looked at his watch. "Better get a move on. Got to make up all the time we lost."

"Lost! I thought that's why we came – to see stuff!"

The family dozed as we chugged through the endless Texas terrain. Toward late afternoon my tornado watch was rewarded.

"Look Mart! A funnel! Can't you drive a little faster?"

His eyes flipped back and forth between the sky and the road. "We'll be fine – if we don't run out of gas. It's still fifty miles to Pecos."

"How did you let it get so low? You have everything else under your control!"

After getting there safely and filling the tank, Mart got back in the car with the look of someone ready to conquer Texas.

"Are we going to stop at Ft. Stockton?" Nick asked. (He'd been studying the map, too).

Mart looked from the darkening sky to his watch. "We can make a few more miles."

We drove along in silence through Ft. Stockton and beyond.

"Mama – Nick hit me," Jeff tattled.

"I'm hungry," Diana complained.

"Let's sing some songs," I said. No one made a sound.

Mart slowed the motor to pass through the town of Sheffield. Stoic Daddy came to life. "Stop! We've driven enough."

I lost all hopes of a fancy motel when I saw the run down tourist court on the edge of town. The only choice. No kitchen. The owner said there was a small café "down the road apiece." As we were cleaning up, Jeanine let out a scream, pointing to the biggest bug any of us had ever seen.

"Everything's big in Texas," Daddy said. Pulling at his chin, he looked warily toward me. "Even trouble."

"No trouble tonight. I was ready to stop, too. At least we won't have to cook."

When I saw the dilapidated building that housed the cafe I almost wished we could. A patch of weeds grew beside the front stoop. The windows were clouded and fly specked. Tables covered with cracked oilcloth. My heart sank.

Pencil poised, the waitress looked at Jeff. "And what would you like little boy?"

"Road apples."

"Road apples are horse-doo, Dummy," Nick said.

"Oh, Joe," Mama scolded. "I told you not to say those things in front of the kids."

Daddy grinned and scratched his head. "They gotta learn."

We were rewarded next day with a stop at The Alamo and our first touch of the tropics at Galveston – where I had it out with Daddy.

"We're not staying in one of these cheap motels again." I was carrying Diana from the bath to the bed – to keep her feet off the dusty floor. Mart and Mama were in the kitchen trying to get the sink to drain.

"Come on," I said to Mart when I'd finished with the kids. "Let's take a walk and get away from this bug brigade."

Daddy shrugged his shoulders and grabbed a cold drink from the cooler. He knew when he was whipped.

Nearing New Orleans next day, I got out the AAA Tour Book and studied the selections. "This motel sounds nice. And it's got air-conditioning."

Next morning – breakfast at Brennan's. I looked around at everyone. "Wasn't it nice having air-conditioning in our rooms last night?"

"Hmmph," Daddy snorted. "I never used the lousy thing."

When breakfast was over we headed north through Mississippi. A stop for gas and rest rooms.

"Mama," Jeanine said. "There's three restrooms here. Men, Women, and Colored. What if our friends from school were here? Wouldn't that be terrible?"

"Yes," I said – powerless to explain.

"Did you hear that kid who waited on us?" Mart asked when we started out again.

"I couldn't understand his southern accent."

"Never been outside the state. Unbelievable. It's only eighteen miles to the Alabama border."

Next morning, we stopped to fix breakfast at a roadside park.

"I'll back the car up to the table," Mart said. "You get out and direct me."

"Keep coming," I beckoned. "Come on. A little closer." Too late.

Mama took one look at the one and only dent in the micro bus. "Come on, kids. Let's go for a walk."

After driving through the Great Smokies, I kept my guidebook open. Making sure we saw Jamestown, Williamsburg, and Yorktown en route to New York. Mart's schedule allowed only one day for New York City, so we hit the major spots. Number one on my list was the Empire State Building. Remembering the elevator at Carlsbad, Mama waited in the lobby, refusing to go up.

"Where's Diana?" I asked, turning from the dramatic view at the top.

"She was here just a minute ago," said Mart.

We went around to the other side. No Diana.

"She must have fallen off," I cried, peering over the ledge.

"Don't be ridiculous. She's got to be here someplace. We'll go in opposite directions."

"We almost lost Diana," I said to Mama back in the lobby.

"We didn't almost lose her," Mart snapped.

"We thought we did. She got away from us and kept going around ahead, till Mart went the other way and found her."

Mama took Diana by the hand. "You'd better stick with me."

Back on the streets we tilted our heads toward the skyscrapered view and gaped like typical hicks. Even so, someone stopped and asked us directions. And Mart knew the answer. He had studied his maps. Later, trying to find Aunt Frieda's house in Danbury, Connecticut, he got lost. No map.

After a pleasant overnight we turned south and began our long trip home.

"Are we almost there?" Diana asked at the first red light.

The three older children understood what they saw at the Smithsonian, the Capitol, monuments, and White House. For Jeff, all that really mattered was the bust of Jefferson Davis tucked away in an obscure corner of the Senate wing. Anyone with a name like that had to be important.

We wended our way through quiet little back roads in rolling green Kentucky. Found ourselves at (Mart steered us to) a forsaken crossing of the Mississippi near Dyersburg, Tennessee. The "ferry" was nothing more than a raft with a fence around it.

"A feller up the river lost a couple cars last week," said the ferryman as we pulled into the whirling current.

Mama set her mouth into a grimace. No one said a word.

"You could've gotten us all killed," I railed at Mart when we got off safely at the bootheel side in Missouri. I could almost hear the click in his mind as he checked off one more sight he had longed to see.

At the Grand Canyon, Mart stopped at the main lookout. "Everybody out for a look. I'll wait here." He'd seen that sight before.

He opted for the slower route to visit Boulder Dam on to Las Vegas, into Death Valley, just on time for breakfast early one morning. The waitress-cook, in the tiny eating place, good humouredly worked her way through eight orders, using her one and only frying pan. We loitered at the souvenirs when we finished eating.

"We better get out of here before the sun gets high," Mart said. "I don't know if our little bus can make it through here in the heat."

Miles down the road I turned to him and asked, "Did you leave her a tip?"

"I forgot."

I clenched my teeth and looked out the window – on through Sonora Pass. The last leg home. Almost there.

A MATTER OF FACT

We were young and poor and had three kids. Nick – the oldest – almost four. After coping with measles, mumps, and chicken pox – three times around – my nerves were shattered. Pop and Mom agreed to baby-sit so we could get away.

"Why are we going to stay at Grandma and Grandpa's?" Nick asked his dad.

"Because your mother needs a rest. I'm taking her away someplace to rest."

We packed their things and headed to South San Francisco where Pop was a preacher. As the pastor's grandkids, they were fussed over after Sunday's service.

"What darling little children."

"Where are your parents?"

Nick looked around for help, but Grandpa was busy at the door shaking hands and giving out hellos. Grandma was in the choir loft pumping out the postlude.

Finally he cleared his throat and stammered out, "They went – they went to their resting place."

CLOSE ENCOUNTERS WITH CARS

"Look at her, Joe. She's driving the wrong way and getting bumped."

Never mind that "bump" is what you were supposed to do in that carnival car. Mama saw through my facade and knew that I had lost control. She stood outside the chest-high wall and watched sparks fly off the trolley-wheel, heard the tires squeal, breathed in the scent of hot rubber, and vowed I'd never get a license. Not while she was in control. It took sixteen years and four kids later before I learned to drive.

For all of Mama's refusal to let me drive, she had learned as a young girl. Sneaking into the garage (out of hearing distance from the house), practicing the gear shifts, slowly backing in and out with Pa's old Model T Ford. At least she had learned the necessary art of control.

Until one night. She was angry at Dad for some reason unknown to my brother or me. She piled us into our black Model A and headed out of town. Eyes blazing, staring straight ahead, she revved the motor faster than we had ever gone. Lucky for us there was no one on the road. Cars were not meant for therapeutics.

Driving and cars mean different things to different people: power, prestige, leisure, necessity, torture. For Grandma they provided thrill. "Can't you make this thing go faster?" she'd ask my brother, barreling down Almond Avenue in our blue Model A. For me they meant independence. Having spent my high school years bumming rides, I was quick to take advantage of my brother's return from World War II and his willingness to drive me places. It didn't take him long to see the value in giving me lessons when Mama wasn't looking.

He would get me out on the highway somehow in Dad's old Plymouth and order me to "Drive." I felt all right going fifty-five. What happens when you have to slow down? I didn't have the feel for controlling the gears and managing the crawl. This was not a carnival or our quiet street. I was petrified.

"Take me to a back road," I pleaded, "so I can learn the gears."

A short lesson in the use of reverse ended in someone's stack of firewood. I was returned to the passenger seat. From there I had a good lesson in road manners listening to my brother rail at the dumb drivers in front of us who didn't move fast enough when the light turned green. To this day I am programmed into fast take offs, trying to escape that imagined diatribe from the guy behind.

Cars come in handy though for honeymoons. Young and poor and car-less, my husband and I borrowed my brother's '46 Nash for a trip up the California coast after our Thanksgiving Eve wedding, 1949. We drove as far as Coos Bay, Oregon, from the San Francisco Bay Area – finding motels without difficulty in this off-season time. The cloudy skies and constant rain had no dampening effect on our high spirits. The crashing waves gave echo of our growing passion. We were glad we had the car.

By 1951 my brother had a new car and invited us to go with him to hunt for the Lost Dutchman Gold Mine in the Superstition Mountains of Arizona in his fancy, red, Chrysler Town and Country convertible. We never found the gold, but we did it up in style.

A few months later we were finally able to purchase a car for ourselves – a 1938 Ford – an adventure in itself when we laid our five month old infant in the back seat in a dresser drawer and headed to Los Angeles to attend Granddad's funeral. Halfway there the old motor sounded off with loud booms and bangs. My husband pulled to the side of the road.

"Get out. Get out," I screamed as I grabbed the baby and ran.

"Come on back," he coaxed. "It's not going to explode.

I climbed inside reluctantly, clutching the baby in my arms, ready to jump out at a moment's notice as we were towed into the small town of Delano. Instead of Granddad's funeral, we spent the weekend in a dismal motel room waiting for the car to be repaired.

Our next car was a red '49 Ford. We didn't have it long. Just long enough for me to win a set of tires for it at some benefit affair – then have to give them up when we replaced the car with a blue and white '54 Plymouth.

They say life begins at forty. For me it began at twenty-nine when I finally learned to drive. A few houses down the street lived a young mother like myself. In spite of the fact that my daughter had chopped off her daughter's hair in a recent game of "beauty shop," the woman took pity on me. She offered to babysit our infant so I could take driving lessons – real driving lessons – from a licensed teacher. It was storybook: a babysitter, professional teacher, and no diatribes. And I learned to drive. The '54 blue and white Plymouth no longer sat beside the house – begging to be driven.

It wasn't long before I was tackling the San Francisco-Oakland Bay Bridge to pick my husband up from work and driving the kids to my parents in the suburbs for homemade donuts and a rousing game of Yahtzee. Mama was glad now that I had learned to drive.

Our teenage kids were glad too when their Dad came home one day with a sporty little '64 red Dodge Dart convertible. The thrill wore off for our oldest daughter when she got stopped by a policeman and given a ticket. She'd been driving around town with the top down – the car filled beyond legal capacity with joy riders. The Dart came in handy a few years later when I drove my son and his bass fiddle to the airport for a youth concert in Scotland. We had rented a wooden case from a local music store for the journey. Someone before us had painted it. We might have been harmless, but we made a crazy sight driving with the top down – an Egyptian mummy perched in back. The much loved red Dart was given a ride itself when the movers drove it into a large van, top down, and filled it with packed boxes for our move to Florida.

Before that though, it shared the garage with our '59 VW Micro Bus. A wonderful little vehicle that couldn't drive too fast – much to my mother's joy as we traveled across the country and back with my parents and four children. A stop one morning to make breakfast in a park produced its one and only dent. The only other mishap the car had on the trip was a cigarette burn, which my Dad left on the back seat. Many years later, after the car was long sold, our son was hitchhiking. Someone in a VW

Micro bus picked him up and he recognized our old car by that burn.

A brand new '62 Dodge van took our family of six on a long drive to the mid-west. Halfway to our destination smoke started pouring out of the motor located between the two front seats. My husband pulled over and hollered, "Everybody out." We all obliged immediately, but soon discovered Diana climbing back inside. When asked why she'd gone back in she replied, "I forgot my zorie," – a cheap dime store rubber sandal.

Later our '68 Buick Station Wagon was the host for many a trip to great hiking areas nearby: Mt. Diablo, Point Reyes Beach, the Dipsy Trail, Livermore Hills, where my friend and I took our kids for outings. More space in the car meant room for more kids. More kids – more fun.

Our brown '73 Ford LTD brought my husband and his belongings from California to Florida where he had taken a new job. Later when Mama came to visit us there, I drove her all around the state showing her the sights: Sanibel Island, where my braking experience came in handy as an alligator crossed the road, Key West, The Everglades, Disney World. As we were driving to Gainesville one day, to see our son at the University, I speeded up my red and white Dodge Aspen to pass a car. Felt mine go in a jerk. The semi that had been sniffing at my tail drew back as the driver witnessed my tire blowing out. Some subliminal message warned me not to bear down on the brake. (This was no alligator crossing!) The speed control was set for sixty. I barely touched the brake. Let the car slow down. Eased it to the shoulder. Stopped. We were still upright!

"You did good," Mama said.

Was that Mama talking about *my* driving?

A few days later a driver behind us in a parking lot began shouting obscenities at me for going too slow.

"Don't talk like that to my daughter," my eighty-year-old mother snapped as she rolled the window down.

"Shhh!" my fifty-year old common sense retorted. "Don't argue with him. He might shoot."

Others have been shot for less on these Floridian roads. The vision of two cars literally fighting on Interstate 95 was still fresh in my mind.

After one too many bad scenes with my Aspen, my husband came home one day with a diesel fueled Mercedes Benz. My elderly friend, who I took for weekly shopping, was doubly pleased to be driven around in that – brown was her favorite color. We liked to include breakfast at Denny's after getting our groceries. One day I discovered the eggs I'd purchased were half cooked from sitting in the hot trunk so long. After that we breakfasted before shopping.

In all my experience with driving and cars I have gotten just two tickets. The first one was for making a U-turn in a business district driving the red Dodge Dart. The other came from speeding around a corner in my black Riviera at 17 miles per hour in a 15 mile-per-hour zone – a speed trap, which had been temporarily posted.

When a car gives me trouble, I remember the heartsick feeling I used to get when I was a teenager during World War II. Gas and tires were rationed. Our car was old and run down. We always held our breath until it started. Perhaps that's why, when someone asks me what kind of car I like best, I always say, "One that runs."

NO SCORE

"Do we have to have her on our team?"

Words I grew up with, always the last one chosen. Never could catch a ball or throw straight. I did okay in those sack races at the annual Sunday School picnic, though I never won a prize. That and running when my mother made me take a May basket to a boy I didn't like. The prize – escaping his kiss.

My athletic talent proved no better when we moved from South Dakota to a small suburban town in San Francisco's Bay Area where grade school classmates vied for top position – crossing hand to hand on iron poles. Bicycles were no easier to handle in spite of my friend Joan's efforts to teach me. I wobbled down the gravel lane from her house to the road. Fear of not reaching the high seat of her brother's bike, looking silly in front of him (he was in my grade), scratched knees, and lack of a bike of my own brought that trip to a halt. I tried again as an adult. My tendency to steer straight for the thing I was supposed to miss overrode any fun I might be having.

Swimming was another unsafe sport. I had learned the dead man's float back in Dakota at the local dam. Tucked into the dry California coastal hills and spattered with green live oak trees, stood Joan's grandmother's house. The big attraction: a swimming pool. A lovely creation formed with plain cement by an artisan's hands. Curves, crescents, smooth rounded edges. Not easy to latch onto. Floundering in the deep end, I grabbed Joan instead. In my panic to stay afloat I held onto to her – pushing her down. Her big brother came to the rescue. I'm looking worse than silly now.

I came alive in high school – learning the rules for football, cheering like the others when Van Brocklin, from my old hometown, scored. I even batted the bird in a game of badminton – trying to impress Bruce – a tall, blond, handsome classmate. I soon copped out (he was practically professional) and joined the school's modern dance group. Isadora Duncan style – bare feet and filmy gowns.

When it comes to spectator sports I haven't done much better. Except for the time the San Francisco Chronicle offered free tickets for Women's Day at the ballpark. My friend Charlotte, brought along a vacuum full of martinis. It saw me through that phase. Afterwards it was all downhill – reaching the bottom when my kids started saying, "Go away, Mom. Don't watch. Our team always loses when you root."

So I opted for washing windows in our three-story house.

"Put your rags away and come play tennis with us," my neighbors called.

Next week I succumbed to them – and tradition – and bought a white tennis outfit. White panties showed seductively. My husband approved. He didn't see my double-jointed arms. Just the panties when I lifted them.

My friends recognized my lack of know-how at first lob. Proper middle class, they accepted me anyway. Until I faltered – falling in a fit of laughter in the middle of the court. Proper attire does not compensate for improper behavior. Next week I received a notice from Montclair Women's Club. Tennis lessons available Monday through Thursday, 8 to 10 am. (Awfully early to be up and dressed – even scantily). I took to writing poems instead.

ACKNOWLEDGMENTS:
"Stir-Fried Memories"

A French Revolution, The Pegasus Review
A Rose is a Rose is a Rose, Spiritual Life
A Matter of Fact, Christian Reader
Back From the Brink, "Hope Whispers," Whispering Angel Books
Carnival, Good Old Days
Catching the Ring, Henderson, Health Clinic
Close Encounters With Cars, Spralopolis
Dear Doctor, Messages From the Heart, Personal Narratives, Hayworth Press, Inc., Caring Stories, PublishAmerica
Fleeing Floyd, Seven Seas
Florida Living, Something to Read
For the Birds, Sprawlopolis
Garage Sale, Nostalgia
Good-bye Again, Black Medina
How's My Backhand?, Vista
I Bring My Book ...., Dorothy Parker's Elbow, Warner Books
La Bomba, VQonline
Paper Moon, The Real Eight View
Prime Time, Inspirit
Making Babies, "Dry Bones Anthology," Dry Bones Press, Inc.
Mama's Move, "Heart By Heart," iUniverse, Inc.
Miss "H", "Gifts From Our Grandmothers," Crown Publishers, "Living Lessons," Whispering Angel Books
Moving Along, "Sacred Stones," Adams Media
No Score, Vintage Northwest
Scattered Beads, Cahoots
Shoreline, Ancient Paths
Stir-fried Genes, "Familiar," The People's Press
The Art of Receiving, The Lutheran Digest
The Fellowship of Women, Lutheran Women
Tide Pools, "Sacred Waters," Adams Media
War Torn, "Palo Alto Review," Bombshell, OmniArts, LLC
What If?, "Personal Narritives," Hayworth Press, Inc.